Dr. Trixie's

PRESCRIPTIONS

by Katharine M. Hikel

Versions of these essays were originally published in
Vermont Woman and *Seven Days.*

Book design by Sylvie Vidrine

Copies of this book are available at Amazon.com

First Edition
2007
ISBN-13: 978-0-979357-10-7

Printed in the U.S.A. by
Morris Publishing
3212 East Highway 30
Kearney, NE 68847
1.800.650.7888

For my beloved family, and to the memory of my mother.

"Equality of rights under the law shall not be denied or abridged by the United States or by any state on account of sex."

~ the Equal Rights Amendment

TABLE OF CONTENTS

Part One: Mother From Hell

Stretch 3
Dumboree 5
Retox 7
Bad to the Bone 9
Natural 12
Let it Bleed 16
Perv 18

Part Two: Doctor From Hell

Time Has Come Today 23
The Pause 25
Out 27
Free The Top 40-D 30
Get It While You Can 32
Shattered 34
Speak, Mammary: The Breast Interview 37
Motherhood In Paradise 41
That Clinking, Clanking Sound 43
Oh Happy Day 46
Past Medical History 48
Cheers 51

Part Three: Dr. Trixie's Prescriptions

Baggage 57
The Cure 59
Let Them Eat Wedding Cake 61
The Bare Necessities 63
Blinded With Science 66
Changing Hands 68
Wired 70
The Watch 72
Coming Home 74
Revolution, Evolution 76
In Memory 78
In Season 81

PART ONE

Mother From Hell

Stretch

My girlfriend Dr. J called me up, ecstatic. She has four children, six grand-children, and a busy medical practice. She knits; she takes photographs for her husband's books; she lifts weights; she's strong and smooth-skinned with lovely legs and the black leather miniskirt to go with them. What made Dr. J so happy? Surgery. Cosmetic. The receiving end. "I had them remove all traces of my children," she gloated.

After the weight gain of a normal pregnancy, it's true – you pucker. I know a woman, a world-class cyclist with two Tours de France under her amazing thighs, who suffered a blowout when a pregnancy with twins split her rectus abdominus muscle – the one that makes up the two halves of your six-pack. She was disheartened by this, and by the ripply softness over her once drum-tight belly. She no longer wears a bikini to the beach, and was astonished when I showed up in mine, pleated and jellied as I am around the belly-button.

I've had other people express astonishment at my thing for string, but I attribute that to living in Vermont, a landlocked state where the biggest lake is full of toxic chemicals and lampreys, and people's idea of swimwear is a baggy T-shirt, baggy shorts, and Tevas, for crawling around in icy glacial streams. Not what any normal person would wear to lie on a real beach, or swim in real salt water, or flirt with real French-Canadian gentlemen in microbriefs like you can on the coast of Maine, where I received my training.

Back home, on the cordless, another girlfriend freaked out when I told her I was out in my own front yard by my own plastic slip'n'slide, in my bikini. "You wear a bikini?" she gasped. "Don't you have stretch marks?"

Of course I have stretch marks, I snapped. Jeez Louise. Would I stop wear-ing lipstick just because I have fillings in my teeth? Would I stop using glitter hair products from K-Mart just because I have white streaks in my bangs?

Besides, stretch marks and other scar tissues look a lot better oiled and browned than they do all mushroom-pale and boggy. The same, I believe, goes for people in general, and older people in particular. Dames of a certain age, as the French say.

And, as one of the guys on a renowned local building crew put it: If you're gonna be fat, you gotta be tan. Tell me construction workers don't know what's hot when it comes to exposure, fashion sense, and covering up defects with a visually pleasing facade.

The good thing about stretch marks, along with silver hair, is that a person can finally walk around half-naked on any beach and not get hassled. No more hey-baby-kissy sounds. No more hornball weirdos trailing me down the dunes. Now I get tanned old greyhaired guys nodding with respect. And women of my age-cohort grinning like conspirators. We are the Woodstock One generation. We practically invented nudity. And we still rule, by numbers if nothing else.

It's encouraging to read all the new studies that show that full-frontal, bare-naked George Hamilton Classic tanning gives us the vitamin D we need to stave off autoimmune disease, cancer, arthritis, depression, psoriasis, osteoporosis, and that ghastly fluorescent pallor that makes a lot of us northerners look like we spent the winter on the underside of a log. I believe in preventive solar therapy, just as I believe that red wine cuts cholesterol, dark chocolate is an antioxidant, and the flouride in the gallons of iced tea that I swill all summer long will protect my teeth.

Furthermore, a Buddhist friend told me that lying naked in the sun is considered the highest form of meditation. Of course. Have you ever seen a Buddhist monk with tan lines?

And it feels good, being nude, or nearly so, after a winter of heavy boots, heavy socks, earflaps, and polyfleece. Though I do admit being brought up short by a youngster at a local beach who, when I was sporting my thong, paddled by me on a noodle chanting, "Wedgie! Wedgie!" Poor ignorant underexposed provincial little thing.

And what's the big deal? Stretch marks are nature's tattoo. You go through a lot to get them. No denying it, no undoing it, no going back. Removal is expensive and not always satisfactory. In any case, you'll never be the same.

The silvery scar tissue doesn't tan perfectly. The bottoms I favor for maximum exposure aren't very supportive. Not a custom fit. A little bulge, a little pooching out. At 53, I don't care. It's not how you look, it's how you feel. Be nice to me or I'll take my top off.

A feature story in *National Geographic* showed pictures of women in the centuries-old matriarchal realm of Rana Tharu, fishing, threshing grain, smoking bidis, and wearing bejeweled crop tops over low-hung skirts expressly designed to show off their stretch marks — evidence of their status as life-bearers and producers. These gals know what's what. Maybe I could move to South Nepal and let it all hang out with them.

No fear. Stretch marks of America, come out and be counted.

Dumboree

I know the Good Mothers have been going on behind my back about my send-ing Baby J off to playgroup with paid help, or – hah – with her father, so that I don't have to do it. Maybe I'd go if they'd talk about something other than bowel function and head lice. Isn't anyone having an affair, or engaged in some other interesting grownup activity, like insider trading? They could at least not blanch and look horrified if I use the words 'multiple orgasm' in a sentence. One does crave acceptance.

And I do, on the whole, like Baby J's company, and I know she should be practicing social interactions, like staggering up to guys and snatching their Frookies, or ramming them with a push-cart if they're cute. But the notion of bonding with people simply because I'm bred and lactating makes as much sense as bonding with them because I have pierced ears and I snore.

Meeting people with whom you share the repetitive boredom and grubbi-ness of the id-development stage is like meeting people in jail, or in the trauma unit. We have something terrible in common at the time, but other than that, our paths would never cross. Mostly because I'd be spending all my time alone, in the back stacks of the biggest library I could find, taking a nap.

Still, I have fits of desperation for grownup company – someone besides my therapist; someone whose idea of a literary reference goes beyond 'SOME PIG'; someone who could maybe use words like 'postpartum psychosis' in a sentence. So when an actress I know, a theater major, a literate, literary person, invited me and Baby J to visit a local baby-gym franchise with her and her small daughter, I accepted.

The playgroup that I weasel out of is in an old tall drafty battered room in our town hall where people also vote, take T'ai Chi and drawing classes, and buy books at the Fourth of July sale. There is a good collection of baby equip-ment and playthings that are sturdy, durable, well-used and well-maintained. There are a couple of tumbling mats, a crawl-through tent, and a climb'n'slide structure. Basic. Serviceable. Plenty of room to run around, and the acoustics make it quite gleeful: toddler yelps and whoops ringing off the high ceiling, and plastic wheels rumbling over an old wood floor.

But this place – wow. Big windows, clean bright walls, fresh paint and new carpet. Floor mats throughout. Things to ride. Things to swing. Things to climb, designed for every developmental level at about three-month increments. Good light. Good music – it sounded like Buckwheat Zydeco. A dozen women, with maybe fifteen kids and two staffers. After ten minutes or so, the children had run around and marked their turf. Everybody's shoes and sweaters were off, two mothers were swing-dancing on the mats, another was singing harmony, and we were just getting warmed up when a staffer called everybody into a circle for the Program.

I hate circle time, especially for babies. It's manipulative. It's stultifying. They'll get enough of it in school. And this one was shameless – a lowbrow interactive commercial with rhymes and jingle-singing about the corporate logo, on a par with that purple dinosaur we all love to hate. The kids mostly looked bored and resigned, except for one or two little suckups who were obviously desperate for approval. I sat there in appalled shock. My girlfriend looked a little embarassed; so did most of the other mothers who were half-heartedly singing and clapping along.

After five minutes, Baby J pointed to the door and shouted, "GO!" We hustled out of there with relief that we neither paid for the visit, purchased any of the overpriced merchandise on the display rack, nor signed up for six more weeks of The Program.

Later, shredding croissants at the donut shop, I wondered: why do mothers cooperate with this relentless dumbing-down? Would the programmers get away with it if the attending parents were a bunch of guys? Is this why guys don't go? Doesn't anyone notice how bored and vacant-looking the kids are? Or is that just the normal habitus of cable spawn? Or is this how we get them all zoned out and ready for school?

On the way home, we stopped by the university dairy farm, where we could romp about unhindered as long as we liked, interact with the calves in the solar barn, and get the answers to all our pressing questions about techniques in bovine artificial insemination. Free.

Amid the lowing of the calves, I fantasized about a franchise where people could go and romp with their kids, with good music and song and maybe a dance pro to actually teach something useful.

Maybe they could call it SMART'N'UP.

Retox

Cravings. Like a prisoner in lockdown, a psych patient in isolation, I'm jonesing about all the things I can't do while in charge of a small person in the preschool stage. Some of it is lofty and respectable, like I wish I could read the entire National Book Award list, or investigate my exciting new treatment for perimenopause – you know, Nobel Prize stuff.

But a lot of times it's just wishing for basic dumb fun, like sitting under a cafe umbrella drinking rum and ogling sailors; or lolling on the beach with a boyfriend, toking a skinny; or stretched out by the pool with a bunch of girl-friends sharing a pack of Luckies - old habits I hadn't thought about in years. Stuff I gave up long ago, when I had to clean up and take calculus.

I thought I had my responsible-parent act together, but maybe being around all this id development has affected me. I NEED IT RIGHT NOW. I WANT MORE. Maybe a surfeit of Barbie accessories has reduced me to my lowest common denominator. Maybe I've inhaled too much dryer lint. Maybe it's sleep deprivation, from being bumped awake every night by a little somebody crawling into my bed for comfort, or by my own bizarro aging biorhythms.

Anyway, one morning when the sun came out after weeks of gray skies and fractured dreams, I said OK when my daughter begged to go out and stomp worms in the driveway. It was about eight o'clock. I put a sweatshirt over my PJs and sat on the back stoop watching her, and soaking up the strange warm sun. Then I realized that I was starving.

I'd slept so badly that I was too tired to even cook an egg, so I piled a huge fistful of the ground round I'd bought for dinner onto a slab of bread. Too tired to make coffee or tea – and I'm speaking truth here – I grabbed by the neck the bottle of Shiraz I was saving for my one glass at dinner, and – too tired to pour – carried it outside.

Sitting there unwashed, uncombed, eating raw meat, and washing it down with a slug from the bottle while supervising a child, I realized what this might look like to a civilized person. Or a social-services worker.

I wondered: is anyone else out there doing this? At 25 I might have worried. Lately, what you see is what you get.

I was relieved, however, when a girlfriend stopped by, and, upon hearing my description of breakfast, said that she, too, had stepped up her intake since her last child was born. A bottle of wine every two days. Pitiful, considering what we used to do in our undergraduate years. Still, we could see what was happening.

My own dear mother used to shriek, "You kids are driving me to drink!"

My esteemed friend and colleague Dr. J, a renowned childrearing expert, said, "Oh, I got through all those years of staying home playing Candyland by smoking a whole lot of anything that was lying around."

My upscale friends hired au pairs, and went off to work till the kids hit middle school. None of them has any substance issues whatsoever.

The medical literature reports a correlation between mothering – the undervalued, underpaid, endless attending to the needs of others over one's own – and higher rates of depression in women. This is undoubtedly why God in her wisdom gave us Prozac. Xanax. Jose Cuervo. Mother's little helpers.

Those using the do-it-yourself approach always have the twelve-step safety net if things get out of hand. Another girlfriend says, "I spend more time going to AA meetings than I ever did going to bars, but it still gets me out of making dinner."

The other bummer is that just as some of us are ready for replacement therapy, our tolerance plummets. Sure, you can chug a glass of mid-morning merlot, but you'll need a 3-hour nap afterwards. And wake up with a headache.

Our mental status wants to be toasted to oblivion, but our metabolism screams for mercy.

And prescriptions for midlife marijuana aren't going to happen any time soon. Which is too bad, because the market would be huge, according to my consumer analysts.

So we're back to basics: a little caffeine, a little pharmacology, a little dilute ethanol. It's like being an adolescent again. You're aware of the limits, but you long to exceed them.

This remembrance of the past may be what gives us the wisdom to act when our kids start messing with the same stuff in their teens.

Like shaking them down periodically to see if they've got anything good.

Bad to the Bone

The only thing worse than being around my own children when they're misbehaving is being around someone else's.

We recently entertained a sub-juvenile offender. He wasn't invited; his mother called and asked us to take her husband and little Beelzebub out of her hair so she could finish her PhD dissertation. We were having a dinner party and egg hunt that evening, so it was convenient all around.

Little Beelzebub had been a handful from the moment they wiped the meconium off his screaming face. He never slept. He projectile-vomited. He was a nipple-biter. He ate bugs. He pulled hair. He painted with poop. He was smart; he was cute; I thought he had potential; but of course he was hauled off to long-term daycare the minute he spat squash into the eye of the last babysitter who could tolerate him. He was kicked out of one program, after the teachers videotaped him as a bad example. In the next, he spent most of the day in solitary. By now he was a hardened criminal – cynical, rebellious, allergic to authority. He'd just turned six.

My kids couldn't stand him. My twelve-year-old barricaded his room so Beelzebub wouldn't destroy it. My five-year-old armed herself with a hockey stick. "In case he pinches me again," she explained.

His father is a likeable, patient guy with an incredible tolerance level.

My partner and I were setting up the egg hunt when Beelzebub and his dad arrived – an hour early. I made my kids take him outside. When I looked out, he was pulling the tail off the kitty. Then he turned on the hose, and drenched the towels that were almost dry on the clothesline.

His father sat on the porch sipping a beer, admiring the view.

The other guests included two well-brought-up, polite little girls, Lily and Rose. By the time they arrived, Beelzebub had pocketed half the hidden eggs. My daughter was following him around yelling, "YOU'RE SUPPOSED TO WAIT!"

Every five minutes, somebody yelled, "MOM!" in a tone of outrage and disbelief about something Beelzebub had done to a kid, a bicycle, the pruning shears, a frog, a swing, my flowers, or the old dog from next door.

I waited.

His father was chitchatting about a book he'd read on the politics of Serbia.

We set the kids up in the library for dinner. My children set the table with their favorite silver and china from the secondhand stores. Candles were lighted. The adults settled in the dining room. All was quiet for twenty minutes. Then there was a yell, and a crash.

When I went in, Beelzebub's plate was on the floor, the cider was knocked over, there was a smoking hole in the tablecloth, and Lily and Rose were on the floor, sitting on the boy, who screamed at the top of his lungs while my daughter poked him with her foot and my son tried valiantly to extinguish the mess.

I said, "Thank you," to the girls, who went quietly back to their seats and put their napkins back on their laps.

Beelzebub was making an tremendous fuss about his bloody nose. I gave him an ice pack, then helped my daughter to her seat, reminding her that it's not considered sporting to kick someone who's already down.

I then grabbed the whining Beelzebub in the wrist lock described by Miss Manners in her "Guide To Rearing Perfect Children," directed him to his chair, and hissed through my teeth, "Now. These are the house rules. No hitting, no hurting, no pulling hair, and no messing up the table. So straighten up and fly right, or I will let these kids sit on you any time they want."

I went back to dinner. "They're fine," I said. Dessert was served and a movie watched with no further incident.

Beelzebub's mother called the next day. On the attack.

"Thank you for including the guys in your party." she began. "Beelzebub said he tried to have a good time, but the kids were mean to him. He has cat scratches all over his arms. He has a burn on his finger. I didn't think that children usually went unsupervised around animals and lighted candles."

"Oh, my," I replied.

She was just getting warmed up. "His nose bled all night. He said the kids ganged up on him, then he said you squeezed him. I should have told you that I don't approve of other people touching my child. The school says he already has issues around personal space."

She suggested, "You could have given him a time-out. He's in it so much at school that I never wanted to do it, but lately it's the only thing that gets through to him."

Then she got to the good part. "I've been thinking that he's just not getting enough one-on-one, so I'm taking the summer off to spend with him before he starts first grade." Hallelujah. This was what the poor kid wanted all along. I wondered how she'd be able to stand him; but she'd already thought of that.

"I was hoping we could get together with our kids and hang out."

"Maybe," I lied. My kids would refuse; and even I didn't want to spend time with a kid who could ruin a day at the beach.

She concluded, "But he said he didn't want to be around you any more, because you're scary."

Whew, I thought. I'm off the hook.

Then it hit me. I'd done the same thing everyone else did to him. I blew him off because I didn't like his style. I didn't bother to engage. I trumped him with authority.

In the adult world, I go out of my way to avoid the kind of people my partner calls "energy suckers." But doing that with a kid who's headed down the wrong path is taking the easy way out. That village that it takes to raise a child isn't just for the easy ones.

Okay, Beelzebub, boy, you're on. Come back, and we'll try it again.

Natural

I hadn't been skinny-dipping in ages.

The last time was years ago, during a full moon in July, in the Atlantic Ocean off the coast of Maine. A girlfriend and I were walking along Crescent Beach that night, after working a long day in the hospital. The sand was still warm, holding the heat of the day. The tide was full; the moon laid out a path of light in the water. We hadn't planned to swim; we didn't have suits; we just peeled off our clothes, stashed them by a log, and dived in like seals. As we swam the moonlit path, in the warm waters brought north by the Gulf Stream, the sea broke in brilliant swirls, lit up by the phosphorescence of millions of tiny organisms whose chemistry was catalyzed by the oxygen of our strokes. It was like swimming in a river of fairy dust.

After that, times were tough. I lived for a while in a condo village with a pool where bathing suits were required; even a classic string bikini was pushing it. When I eventually moved to the country, I could sunbathe au naturel to my heart's content, but the only water around was a leech-infested farm pond, or a couple of glacial mountain streams where you had to wear shoes and clothes just to keep your skin from being ground off against the rocks. And there was one interactive episode with a security guard at a public beach on Lake Champlain, who threatened action if I didn't put my top back on – because there were children around. Weren't breasts, after all, invented primarily for children? Another crushing reminder that the Woodstock era was dead and gone.

Some time after that, on a sweltering summer day, I was invited to meet a friend and her children at a pond I'd heard about – a small reservoir surrounded by footpaths through tall pine trees and young hardwoods, which never seemed to be patrolled by any authorities, and where swimsuits were optional. Here was the chance I'd been waiting for. I packed up my toddler and our lunch, and we were off.

My friend Marisa was visiting from Texas, and I was glad to see her. We had known each other since the birth of my son, two years earlier; she had been my midwife, guiding me in all the preparations and traditions of home birth. We'd hit it off, and had remained friends. She was smart, fun, and good to be with. She had great hands; her prenatal exams were like massage therapy. She made all sorts of things with those hands: clothing, furniture, flowerbeds, big productive gardens. She could shear sheep; she could spin, knit, and weave. She foraged for wild greens and mushrooms. She baked dense, grainy breads. She was, of course, a vegetarian; we diverged on some points, but I recognized her discipline and dedication in her intent to live in reverence for life. And she didn't nag me too much about my own less energetic approach. She compounded her own herbal medicines, many of which I enjoyed, steeped as they were in 100-proof ethanol; the timely application of a few drops of echinacea pickled in hi-test vodka worked, I thought, pretty well during cold-and-flu season.

She knew all the flora that grew in abundance around the pond, and told me their names as we walked along the path. St. John's wort. Plantain. Jewelweed. Motherwort. Yellow dock. Camomile. All weeds that I'd mostly ignored my entire life. There were signs of plentiful wildlife – porcupine, muskrat, deer – and the chattering of birds; and there were no automobiles, boats, or ATVs. It was clean and serene, and it was the middle of the week, so there were no other people around. We found a spot on a gentle slope down to the water where our kids could play, spread out our blankets and opened our lunch baskets.

Marisa had brought raw vegetables, whole-grain bread, and some kind of spread made with chopped-up tempeh or tofu, or both. She wouldn't eat anything that had eyes. I'd brought tuna on rye, plums, and chocolate cookies from the supermarket bakery. I could see that she was a little annoyed when her kids hovered over my stash, helping themselves to forbidden pleasures. I said that it was on her account that I'd left the salami at home.

The children took off their clothes and played in the water. Marisa and I took off our clothes – she dressed in breezy cotton dresses, and never wore underwear – and lounged on the blanket, sipping iced tea (herbal, with honey, for her; Lipton, with sugar, for me). We are both olive-skinned and sun-loving, as Mediterranean women often are. Her hair, dark like mine, was longer, and her smooth skin browner; she's taller and slimmer than I, and supple and flexible from decades of yoga. We talked and basked in the sun, rubbing oil into our bare skins – a homemade comfrey and olive oil blend for her; Bain du Soleil for me. She told stories about her work – about teaching prenatal yoga in Spanish; about slipping a loop of umbilical cord from around a baby's neck as its head emerged; about using her capable hands to massage and hold a birthing woman's perineum so that she could deliver a ten-pound baby with no cutting or tearing – and teaching these skills so they will not be lost, in this age of technological intervention.

Our children were wrapped up in their play, the older ones supervising the youngest. Marisa, on her blanket, showed me some warm-up yoga stretches, and demonstrated a couple of advanced poses, which I could barely manage, my blanket sliding down the slope as I cranked my ears toward my knees where they were never meant to be. She moved from one pose to the next smoothly, effortlessly, like a dancer. She was all leanness and muscle – not ripped, like a gym rat, but supple, like a cat. Then she stood up, stretched her lovely bare self, and looked at me with another challenge. "Race you across the pond," she said.

Oho, I've got her now, I thought. No contest. I'm a strong recreational swimmer. I've trained in the ocean; I swim indoors in the winter; I can rip off a mile in the lake without thinking about it. Marisa had spent the last year teaching midwifery in a clinic in El Paso. The desert. Dry, hot, arid. I'd heard about the conditions there from another friend: "Brown dirt, brown grass, and the only blue water's in the toilet bowl."

Marisa can't be in any shape for this, I thought. "You are on," I said.

We told the kids to time us. We dived in. The water was silky, brown, fragrant. I love being naked in water, outdoors. A Zen friend once told me that sunbathing nude is considered to be the highest form of meditation; but I think nude swimming is. The water felt like a whole-body caress. I stayed under, dolphin-kicking as the Olympians do to get an easy lead; I came up, figuring she'd be well behind me, but no – there she was by my ear, freestyling away. A little choppy, but moving right along.

She can't keep that up, I thought. We were barely a quarter of the way across.

I'm a breast-stroke specialist, and I kicked it up into about second gear, going smoothly along and prolonging my glide under water, which I knew would keep me ahead with little effort. After about ten strokes I broke and looked around – there she was again, flailing a little more, but still right off my shoulder. She had to have been doing road work or something, back there in Texas. She was much faster than I thought.

I slowed down a little to let her get ahead so I could watch. Her stroke was messy; she was plonking her arms all over the place, and breathing awkwardly toward the front, but her cadence was steady, and she wasn't even winded. She made a wake like a motorboat.

I let her keep a slight lead to what I guessed was the halfway point, then I brought it on. As I passed, I looked at her; we both grinned, and then I saw something in her face that said she was seriously into this challenge. She charged ahead, and I suddenly found myself having to work to keep my lead. We had about thirty yards to go.

Then she screamed.

And then she went under.

I treaded water furiously for a few seconds, trying to figure out where she was. She broke the surface with a gasp, yelled again, and streaked for the shore.

I lit out, staying slightly ahead – this still being a race – but switching to free-style so I could keep my eye on her over my shoulder. She plowed through the water like a woman possessed.

I touched the shore, and stayed in, treading water; she pulled up a half-second behind me, panting. She clambered onto a big rock, and bent over, inspecting herself Down There.

"Oh, my God," she wailed, "I'm bleeding."

Wow, I thought. This is the most dramatic onset of menses that I have ever seen.

"Something bit me," she said.

I dogpaddled in for a closer look. Sure enough, a trickle of blood meandered down her inner thigh from somewhere in the raven curls of her bush. I saw the glint of something metallic, and leaned in to see.

"Whatever can that be?" I said, pointing. She grimaced, and showed me: a tiny, shiny, silvery-purple labial ring pierced her dusky outer lip. A spot of fresh blood welled up nearby.

"Oh. My," I said. It was my first genital piercing.

"We had a slow day at the clinic a while ago," she explained. "It seemed a good time to practice sterile technique. We all did them on each other." You get a unique view of the world when you are working constantly Down There, as midwives do.

"I see," I said. So did some innocent little pond creature – a turtle? a frog? a fish? – who found the bling appealing, and went in for a nibble.

"You've got the right lure," I said. "Your trolling speed was probably a little too fast."

We paddled back to our picnic. The kids said we'd done the half-mile in about thirty minutes, which was not bad for a nursing mother and an inhabitant of the Chihuahuan desert.

Ever since that day, whenever I go skinny-dipping, I take off everything. I mean everything – jewelry and all. Because you really don't know what's out there. Waiting.

Let it Bleed

The countdown years. At some point you start to wonder – how many menstrual periods do I have left? The monthly flow becomes a reassurance, a blessing, a postponing of the next inevitable step.

Bleeding, though, is a troubled word. We allow the bloodshed of violence and war – men's bleeding – but shun the simple blood of the moon and of childbirth.

We're far removed, by our religions, by our education, from the reverence for physical processes that were once considered holy. It's thought that humans' first concept of time arose from our ancestors' noting that their menstrual rhythms matched those of the moon.

But the bleeding. Maybe we could call ours something else, to distinguish it from the blood of violence and injury. The names we use and hear are so inaccurate. 'The curse.' 'Moon time.' 'Period.' 'On the rag.' 'My visiting friend,' they used to say. None of 'em comes close.

The tides are more like it. Gravity. Something in waves you can't always predict or control, despite records of synchronized cycles among women who live together, influenced by light or pheromones.

It's a cultural thing, too. North Americans are told that a normal flow is five to seven days, and so it is. Europeans expect three to five days, and they get it. In East Africa, it's one or two days. One legendary resident of Berkeley, California, was said to have consciously reduced her flow to a couple of hours while she was squatting in her garden.

Maybe we should have a variety of words for our bleeding, the way we have a variety of words for clouds and weather. The slow mellow flow that slides out nice and easy: Love Paint. The three-days-late one that has you in a cold sweat waiting for it to arrive: Mercy. The achy-breaky, hurty kind that makes you hug the hot pad: Hold Me. The pulsing roaring back-arching kind that takes your breath away and is a precursor of what you'll know in childbirth: The Teacher.

It's astounding that over half the population experiences this as a matter of course through most of our adult lives, yet we have no vocabulary for it. It's unmentionable. Taboo.

The uterus is perhaps the most powerful muscle in the body. It does its hardest work while stretched to its greatest capacity. Yet we do our best to ignore it, deny it, keep it out of our consciousness.

Hysterectomy – named from the days when the uterus was thought to travel around the body, causing hysteria – is still one of the most common surgeries in the U.S. A doctor girlfriend of mine insists on calling it "uterectomy" – one small step to restoring truth in patient relations. No doubt it'll be a while before the rest of managed care catches on.

In other systems, the womb is part of the lower chi, or the second chakra, connected with power, responsibility, wealth and sexuality. The guardians of these forces – priestesses, herbalists, midwives, and anyone who dealt with abortion – have been historically harassed by church and state. This is, of course, still going on. A whole region of essential anatomy has been demonized.

Most U.S. hospitals still insist on major utero-abdominal surgery for one of every four births, usually blaming the mother for 'failure to progress,' though their standards of progression (one centimeter of dilation per hour; sixty minutes for pushing) are impossible to meet. Our childbirth safety and survival records are among the worst of all the developed nations. Home birth with a midwife – a reasonable, cost-effective consumer choice – is illegal in many states, including New York, and overly regulated in most others. Some hospital-affiliated nurse-midwives, backed by mainstream OB, are trying to prevent practitioners with years of training and experience from even using the title 'midwife.' The uterus becomes battle turf. No wonder it's not working as well as it might.

Psychologically, the bleeding-time is a time of repose and connectedness. Some of us sit on the couch and write letters, or talk on the phone. Our dream life is richer. The old wisdom – "Red Tent" theory – says that the bleeding-time is when women knit society together.

But, in the TV ads, the liquid used to demonstrate absorption of menstrual products is always blue. Red is still taboo.

How do you break the taboo? I love the line in the late Wendy Wasserstein's play "Uncommon Women and Others" where the heroine announces, "I have tasted my menstrual blood."

Relaxing the constraints, however, comes at a price.

In my household, where modesty is a lost concept, my preschool daughter stood by in the bathroom the other day, observing as I attended to my feminine hygiene. She said, "I see it's your bleeding time. Can I unwrap that tampon for you?" While chagrined at the lack of privacy, I was charmed by the offer of help.

When she's twelve, just getting into it, I'll be 59, and well beyond. I wonder how many more chances I'll have to show her about taking care of this major part of herself, this colorful piece of the big story.

Perv

～～

The problem of what to do with sex offenders reminds me of one day when I took my baby to Leddy Beach.

It was hot, with a light breeze for AC. The sky was blue, fluffed with clouds. A few other beachgoers were dispersed along the strand. Mellow beach vibes.

My baby daughter, and her eight-year-old brother and his friend all loved the beach. As do I. I spread out the blanket, sunscreened the kids, distributed toys, and stretched out in my bikini to tan the stretch marks. My children happily occupied themselves within earshot. I settled in for a rest – then I saw him.

He sneaked up quietly; these guys always get a little too close. He sat on the wrong side of the tree next to me – not the sunny side, where he could see the lake, but the shady side, where he could see the rip-rap and crown vetch poking through the wire mesh on the embankment – and me.

He had no towel, no toys. He had a three-year-old boy with him. Poor kid, I thought, shifting a little on the blanket so I didn't have to see them. I should have put a stop to it right there, but I figured I'd cut the kid a little slack. I angled away and closed my eyes.

A couple of minutes later I opened them to check on my children, and there he was, down by the water, standing, so I could see him – right between my legs. The little boy was off to one side, but he wasn't watching the boy. He was watching me.

I sat up and scowled at him, and he moved away. He was youngish – early 30's, maybe – pudgy, not very tall, and out of shape. Furtive. Sheepish. A typical creep. I got up, and strode across the sand to where my kids were.

He got out of my way – without even feigning a polite greeting, which is another sign – and scurried like a rat back to his tree.

Only this time he sat so he could see the water. And me.

I splashed around in the shallows with my daughter, while the boys swam further out. We moseyed down the beach and back; then it was time to eat. We returned to our blanket, where I served sandwiches and chips. During this time, my voyeur moved back to full viewing position, making no effort to hide his stare. His little boy played quietly around his knees. I decided to wait.

My daughter liked a little nursing after lunch, and I was prepared. She curled up in my lap and I draped my pareo over my head and shoulders, shading her face and covering my torso, with my back turned to the creepy dude, and she happily latched on. After a few minutes she was almost asleep, so I leaned sideways and lowered her to the blanket, then stretched out beside her, still covered, still nursing. All was quiet.

Then I heard his voice. In front of me.

He'd moved to the bottom of the embankment, maybe six feet away, and was talking, too loudly, to the boy. His left arm was around the child's shoulders. His right hand was on his own crotch.

I raised myself up on an elbow and said, "If you don't mind. I'm trying to get this baby to sleep. You are sitting too close." I said, "Furthermore, I'm getting annoyed at your sneaking around staring at me." He looked startled, like, who, me? I sat up. "What makes you think I want to look at you every time I open my eyes?"

Then, so help me, I said, "If you want some boobs to look at, go home and look in the mirror."

His mouth fell open, but no sound came out. I shook my finger at him. "THIS is harassment," I said. I couldn't stop. "Do you like it? I don't, and you aren't going to do it around me, so go."

He was backing up, but he said, feebly, "What are you gonna do, beat me up?" It wouldn't have been hard. I could have easily slugged him with my water cooler. I just glared. Finally he crept away. I never saw see him again.

That one was small potatoes. The tip of the iceberg.

I've read enough sex-offender literature to know that there's a whole spectrum of them. Most of them are a psychological can of worms. The worst ones have a terrible cure rate. I don't want them around. I don't care about their civil liberties – why should theirs matter more than mine, and my children's? Tattoo them, brand their faces, so we'll know. Put them into peaceful seclusion. Gently, respectfully geld them – surgical castration is still the only proven remedy for habitual sexual offenders. Zero tolerance.

Yes, they are abused and traumatized themselves; I'm sorry for that. I've also heard too many stories from my sisters and friends and nieces and babysitters about being perved and annoyed and harassed and molested, again and again and again – as waitstaff, as store clerks, as managers, as concert-goers, as students, as professionals, as women walking down the street. I've dealt with it plenty on my own. And now I have a daughter. And now I've had enough.

PART TWO

Doctor From Hell

Time Has Come Today

We are in yet another age of war. Perhaps – one can only hope – we are also on the edge of another wave of feminist activity. By that I mean another look at the position of women as eternal support staff in the all-guy hierarchy of the world of politics, medicine, law, commerce, arts, entertainment, media, need I go on.

I know some people are thinking, Oh, no – not again. The Bitch Manifesto. The hairy legs and armpits. The Society For Cutting Up Men. The endless meetings, support groups, rallies, protests – the whole three-ring media circus. The nonstop critiques of everything we are used to. Why can't everyone just stay home and play nice?

Robin Morgan, the editor of "Sisterhood Is Powerful," said that every culture in every era has had some form of feminist – that is, woman-centered – politic, however hidden. Historically, periods of activism around women's rights and status have followed eras of quiescence. These activist eras have also, historically, been connected to times of war.

The first suffrage movement saw our founding sisters – many of them daughters of the American Revolution – mobilizing for the right to vote. This action coincided with the Civil War. The next wave, in which the gals in white dresses gained us that right, happened around World War I.

During World War II, the war effort was more of a unifying force than any overt feminist politic; but women pulled equal weight, filling in positions everywhere and even creating government-backed food and childcare programs for themselves – until the postwar effort displaced thousands of women workers back into their homes (or onto the street), and into the consumer housewife paradigm of the 1950's.

The last resurgence in women's activism occurred during the Viet Nam war. We broke many of the barriers to equal opportunity – in reproductive rights, in access to jobs and education, in legal rights. The movement died – probably of shock – with the astonishing failure of this country to adopt the Equal Rights Amendment (first proposed in 1923), which states: "Equality of rights under the law shall not be denied or abridged by the United States or by any state on account of sex." People kept saying that the country was "not quite ready" to guarantee women constitutional rights equal to those of men.

Then along came the Reagan years, a free-for-all of acquisition for the haves, while those of us in the underfunded women's health clinics were choking under the Gramm-Rudman gag rule – designed by men – which tried to keep us from talking about abortion to women in dire straits who really didn't want to be pregnant. That was a ton of fun. Still, lots of women were very busy acting upon our new-found opportunities – getting educated, getting hired, getting elected – in a myriad of ways and styles.

Maureen Dowd, the unfeminist (and the only woman) columnist for the New York Times, recently cited research indicating that, because of our chromosomes, the Y and the X, men are basically all alike, and women are essentially all different.

Or, as Vermont politico John Tracy told me, "There is no women's politic." There's been a lot of distancing from those heady days when Gloria Steinem and the editors of *Ms.* magazine had the cachet of rock stars, and "Sexual Politics" by Kate Millett topped the charts. Anti-feminism, or at least feminist-distancing, is alive and well – mostly because any woman who expects to keep her hard-won job in journalism, in science, in law, politics, any of those things, had better toe the line, not kick up a ruckus – don't upset the Big Guy. 'Cause he's always looking for a reason to downsize the numbers of women, so we won't get all uppity and change things around from the way he's always had them.

Consolidation in woman-centered thinking occurs around wartime, which is also a time of what you could think of as the extreme in excessive male behavior, when a war economy supersedes all the arrangements that we are most comfortable with – like quality education, health care, social security, child-rearing, the environment, our right to supervise the contents of our own uteri, and world peace.

Do fewer of us than before agree upon the importance of these things? I don't think so. Have women, while climbing the ladders of their professions, had to squelch their concern for human-centered issues? I do think so. Have women who are stretched to the max with child care and underpaid jobs and too much housework had their energies diveted from their own constitutional well-being? I know so.

So. The guys in charge get us right where they want us – totally preoccupied with activities of daily living – and what do they go off and create for themselves? More war. Even when we have the diplomacy and the economic edge to talk our way out of it, or to buy our way around it – they don't. They choose war. Is everyone OK with that?

Gentlewomen, start your engines.

The Pause

OK, I admit it. I'm cranky. I wake up nights in a sweat. I can't concentrate on the housework or the grocery list. Sometimes I forget what year this is.

I don't think these problems are health-related.

I am so tired of hearing about menopause. Sure, I'm fifty-something, have white streaks and knee creaks, and can't hear the stereo unless it's cranked. And I want a convertible, and a sizzling affair, and I get dry heaves when anyone invites me to a baby shower. This is a problem?

Anyone who's survived teenhood in America should find menopause a piece of cake. We have licenses; we have credit cards. We have sucked up to all the teachers we are ever going to suck up to. We can drink and smoke and get laid as much as we want. We can lip off at school board meetings, and write letters to the editor. We can vote. What is the problem?

The problem is that just as we reach the pinnacle of our powers, the commercial medical media insists on converting our status into a diagnosis.

Other cultures don't have our symptoms as hallmarks of women getting older. Elsewhere, other stuff happens. In Japan: shoulder pain and a weird taste in the mouth. In other cultures, sexual disinhibition, freedom from child care, and the right to hold public office.

We get hot flashes, night sweats, crankiness, and a steep decline in the feminine art of deference.

These are not symptoms; they are reactions. To what, you might ask?

Let's start with politics. If the tables were turned – if there were 13 men and 87 women in the US Senate; and 35 men and four hundred and something women in the House – we'd see who got hot flashes, mood swings, and crankiness.

Fashion. If men's secondary sex characteristics were covered up, restrained, fetishized, ranked too big or too small, and fed on synthetic hormones and environmental toxins, we'd see who got malignant lumps.

Privacy. If men's major generative organs were debated, voted upon, taken to the Supreme Court, tied to their parents, and constantly made a matter of public opinion, we'd see who developed dysfunctional bleeding.

What I am saying is – this is not a particularly woman-friendly culture.

I hate waking up in a sweat in the middle of the night worrying about war. I'm tired of ads pushing addictive drugs made from horse urine. I wince at

"Race for the Cure" buttons.

The commercial medical cartel – even the women in it – play right into this. They tell us to expect the worst. They look at our experiences as symptoms. They love finding symptoms – this gives them work. They pretend that screening, sympathy and toxic medications are the cure.

Take this pill! Buy my book! Come back for follow-up in two weeks!

Enough about the cure. What about the cause?

Some guy at a local Learning Center is selling classes on so-called Natural Prescription Drugs for Menopause. He's a pharmacist, and a member of the North American Menopause society.

The president of the North American Menopause Society is a man.

The OB-GYN establishment doesn't see anything wrong here. Ninety percent of the heads of OB-GYN departments nationwide are also men.

What year is this? No wonder we are waking up in the middle of the night all heated up.

Women are the major consumers of health-related products and services. We are the cash cows of the medical and self-help industries. The more problems we have, the more stuff they can sell us. Does anyone imagine their really wanting to fix this?

It goes back before menopause. If it's terrible for everyone when we stop bleeding, it's worse when we start. The Great Wall of Taboo surrounds a function that 51% of the adult population experiences for most of our adult lives.

Blood, gore, guts, dismemberment, disembowelment, and decapitation are depicted with astonishing realism in movies and video games - yet the juice they use in the maxi-pad ads is still - blue! As if the worst thing a woman can do is be seen bleeding good old 100% red American blood.

Unless, of course, it's from a severed artery or a bullet wound.

Is everybody comfortable with that?

No? Well, then you probably have PMS. We have the cure for that too! Hormones, antidepressants, and make an appointment to come see me again.

We spend our whole lives trying to cover up our monthly cycles; when they stop, you'd think everyone would be happy. But no. We become the change-over market. This gives us pregnant mares chained together in warehouses so their urine can be condensed into cancer-causing drugs that keep our complexions youthful. Which is THE ONLY undisputed benefit of exogenous estrogen.

So call it something else. Call it post-election syndrome. Call it hypersensitivity to commercial medicine. Call it a reaction to gender unbalance. But stop calling it menopause. That is not the problem.

Out

Lounging in the shade at camp with a cool drink, watching the sunlight on the lake and the kids playing in the water, I asked the young friend sitting beside me how her love life was going.

She grimaced, and shrugged in her hoodie. "You know how it is in high school. If you're a guy, as a freshman, you only date freshman girls. But by the time you are a senior, you can date anyone in any of the classes. And when you're a freshman girl, you can also date in any of the classes; I did a lot of dating in the first three years of high school. But by the time you are a senior, you really aren't looking at younger guys; and as for your classmates, you know everything they've done, everyone they've been with, and so on. It can get a little thick. So I'm enjoying quite a long dry spell.

"But," she said, brightening, "did you hear about Jayzee?"

Jayzee was what you'd call the babe of the 'hood. She and he had been best friends since the diaper era. They didn't go out; they hung out, as kids do in country neighborhoods, with paths between everyone's houses, and kids looking after each other in a casual way. Their younger siblings were a posse, so they were together a lot, and they were adorable together – both tall, good-looking, athletic, smart, funny, and just good to have around.

"Jayzee has found the love of his life," she said. "A terrific guy. Fun, good-looking, and he treats Jayzee really well. They do everything together. Jayzee says, 'I can't stop thinking about him!'" She laughed. "I'm so jealous!"

She looked at me kind of shyly and said, "I didn't know if you knew that he came out."

I'd wondered about that; not about Jayzee himself, but when he would go public. Everybody knew he'd be a hell of a boyfriend.

My young friend mused, "Sometimes I think it's harder being heterosexual than homosexual."

Another friend once put it: "I sympathize with people whose parents freak out because they're homosexual. My parents freaked out because I was sexual."

In this culture, coming out as any kind of sexual is a hard thing for young people. We are still fighting the concept that sex happens after marriage, and marriage happens with a man and a woman, even though biology hardly supports this delusion. And, as with most delusions fostered by adults, it's the kids who suffer.

Like all biological processes, sexuality is a continuum. Its roots are planted in childhood. I knew this when I fell smack in love with Barry D on the first day of kindergarten. I wanted to sit next to him, to touch him, to snuggle up against him and smell his lovely smell. I told my mother I wished I could sleep with him; I didn't know why she was horrified. I was five years old. I meant sleep.

Naturally I wasn't surprised when my son fell smack in love with Maria on his first day of school, and I shared his agony when she cut him stone dead at circle time.

Our culture is paradoxically sexually repressed, and sexualized, and children, with their subterranean radar way tuned in, know what's going on, even about stuff we don't talk about.

So I wasn't surprised when, in first grade, a friend of my son's looked at me shyly and said, "You know, sometimes boys are with boys." I said, "Oh! I am so glad that you mentioned that!" and offhandedly brought up a few boy couples that I knew, and noted the relieved look on his face.

It was in pre-school that a friend of my daughter switched genders – completely, without inhibition, and with the total support of the class, whose members corrected me if I slipped and used the wrong pronoun. It was natural to them that their friend chose the right way to go.

Outside the locker rooms at the gym, I saw another child – this one about ten – redefining gender identity. There was some confusion on the mother's part about which locker room the child should use, but the child was very clear about it, and seemed to have no trouble blending in.

Meanwhile, my friend in the hoodie just wanted to find a guy who'd treat her right.

If we'd take our lead from our children, and let them be as they please, and help them through what's normal and natural instead of forbidding it, then maybe they'd have a chance to find out just what love has to do with it.

In med school, an upperclasswoman took me aside and gave me a list – a very short list – of residents on whose services I should sign up. "These are the dudes," she said. "Having a crush gives you a reason to get dressed and show up for rounds at five-thirty every morning."

I ended up spending ridiculous amounts of time on one particular surgery service. I still feel a warm glow whenever I peek into an OR; I can still tie one-handed knots with either hand, a thing I was taught in an atmosphere of love. Unspoken and unrequited, as it often is in a professional setting – but love nonetheless. Sometimes it's just there, and that's all.

I'm not saying I wouldn't jump at one more chance to shag the daylights out of those gorgeous orthopedic bones. Still, my rule is, better to wish you had than wish you hadn't.

Maybe that's what we should teach our children. Your sexuality — whoever you are, whatever it is — is there; it's a good thing, a natural thing; it's your biology. And sometimes you'll act on it — like Jayzee was lucky enough to do — and sometimes you won't — like my friend in the hoodie.

Sometimes you can come right out. And sometimes you have to wait it out.

Free the Top 40-D

School's in; so are the fashion cops. Vermont schools all make their own dress code rules. Some say that all cleavages, umbilici, and underthings should be hidden, even while current styles favor x-treme exposure.

The rules exist to prevent sexual frenzy, which could distract people from their work. This same attitude lands women under burkhas and chadors; the next thing you know, it's indecent to drive a car, or sit beside a guy in med school.

Wrong attitude. Face it. The human body is here to stay. Get used to it.

Isn't the human form everybody's favorite work of art? And isn't it fun, watching some sweet young thing fish around for his cell phone with his waistband down around his thighs and his pockets at his knees, while trying to hold up that saggy rear with his other hand?

That may be a message of sorts, but I'm not sure it's a sexual one.

Elsewhere, uplift seems to be the goal. At the coffeeshop, all the good-looking counter helpers wear tight, plunging T-shirts over padded miracle undergarments that raise their bosoms to Grand Teton heights. Perfect for sugaring, stirring, ringing up money.

Far different from olden days, when, if you owned a bra, you left it in the drawer and went loose, wild, and free. Nipples were a way of life.

Fashions of the '60's and '70's forged a gap, between us and the generation that told half of us to cover up, and sent the rest off to die in the jungle. The guys in suits who thought up that plan were exactly who we didn't want to be like. Vestiges of these feelings remain, so whenever I see somebody pantsed down to their pubic rami, or hoisted up bold and proud for all the world to admire, I think, Whew, they're not one of Them.

And, even if sexual allure is part of someone's dress code – so what? If you feel you must respond to every vision you encounter, get a grip. Surely you can walk by a row of restaurants without having to taste everything on the menu. Even if you are hungry.

The myth that humans are mad animals with uncontrollable sexual urges is mostly fantasy (go ask the makers of Viagra). The few odd nutballs out there with uncontrollable sexual urges do have a problem, and should see a surgeon. The rest of you may just put your eyeballs back into your heads, and mind your manners.

Guidance counselors and vice-principals who blanch at bra straps and belly-buttons may be suffering other pangs. Surely, after all those power lunches, we are no longer fitting into those low-slung minis we wore to see Cream. Surely, after all those babies, we aren't the perky silhouette we used to be, dancing in the moonlight.

Face it – we aren't getting Those Looks, even if we are going to Vicki's Secrets and jamming our 40DD's into the slinkiest underwires money can buy. And we wouldn't, even if we got all that smooth young flesh covered up, thus leveling the playing field. Because our time is past. Theirs is here.

But we have obligations. Our assets may be repositioned, but we still have to manage them. That is why God in her wisdom invented the gym pass. Spandex. Bud Lite.

Maintenance is half the job. The rest is, I think, to guarantee the freedom of our young to adorn their bootie however they please, without interference. This will allow them to concentrate on the important stuff.

Like, how to run the world.

Get It While You Can

It was the first day of Human Sexuality class in medical school, a very yang-oriented production. We watched a film about pornography, and reviewed erectile and ejaculatory physiology. Typical guy stuff, as usual.

My esteemed friend and colleague, Dr. J., a former midwife with four home-birthed children of her own, turned to me and hissed, "I wish they'd tell the truth about post-partum sexuality."

Still in the pre-child era myself, I smartly remarked, "Huh?" I could see that, after pushing a fully-formed human being through a passage that ordinarily accommodates a pinky-sized tampon, a little R&R might be nice. Still, the textbooks and lectures told us that intercourse can be comfortably and safely resumed within weeks of a normal vaginal birth. 'Proceed with caution' was the only counsel I'd heard. I didn't then comprehend the problem with post-partum sexual activity.

"There isn't any," she announced, in what I recognized retrospectively as the Voice of Wisdom.

I was shocked at the time, because Dr. J. was the kind of person who wore black leather miniskirts, drove a red convertible, and didn't seem as though her sexuality had ever been impaired by anything. And, she'd obviously done something to get the four kids, one after another.

"Just you wait," she said.

I recalled this truth during the bleary era of all-night breast-feeding, followed by the cling-on toddler years. 'Give it to me right now' is the first thing babies learn. Anyone who's been through this knows how it feels to be occupied territory. The last thing I wanted was another set of hands groping me, especially when I could be using the time to sleep. Still, I was often desperate enough to trade sexual favors for a few moments of adult company, even if it mostly consisted of panting and moaning.

I did not then realize that the post-childbirth period of restricted sexual activity would last throughout the entire span of years it takes the fetus to achieve legal adulthood.

A parent's sexual interest often resumes around the first time the child sleeps through the night. In my family this typically occurs at four to six weeks — and then not again until fifteen. I mean years.

Oh surely, you say, you've had the luxury of putting them to bed early, then crawling in for a little nookie with your partner who's been keeping the bed all warmed up.

Not in my house. I'd Mother Goose the daylights out of them, leaving them in a deep drooling coma – up from which they would pop like toadstools after a rain, the minute any pre-sexual impulse began to stir in my limbic system.

Or, they go down like a stone then wake up screaming with the ear-thing just as you've retrieved the vial of scented massage oil from under the bed.

Or, it doesn't even get that far, because while you are waiting in freshly laundered sheets with the candles lighted, your mate has fallen fast asleep in the kid bed, under the spell of juvenile literature.

A 1993 study on sexuality and couples said that one of the main factors associated with sexual inactivity is the presence of children. This research supports my theory that children are pre-programmed to inhibit any event that could engender more siblings. They stifle any competition before it is conceived.

Every parent-set I've ever heard of sneaking off for "Private Time" or "A Little Nap" reports a 95 to 99 percent interruption rate. One desperate couple I know hired a sitter to take the babbie out of the house so they could hook up for a nooner. It's amazing that anyone ever produces a second child under such duress.

A 1997 study on marriage and sex reported that the greatest predictors of sexual satisfaction for both men and women are being in relative good health – and staying sexually active. So. We have to have it. They don't want us to. It's them against us.

These pathetic circumstances have spawned what is known as the Mc-Quickie, below which I hope I never have to go.

From my research, however, I can prescribe the best method for overcoming prolonged postpartum sexual dysfunction: Go away. A quiet, secluded weekend in a hotel with four-foot-thick walls and a "Do Not Disturb" sign works well, especially if it's in the middle of Manhattan, where they will never find you.

Another successful escapade was a recent college reunion – my 30th, if that's any clue to how long I have lived a life of quiet desperation. Strolling around the quads and dorms where I made my first forays into the world of foreplay, it dawned on me: thirty years later, I still have to leave home in order to be sexually active.

Event tickets, lodging, and meals: hundreds. Weekend live-in child-minders, meals, movies: more hundreds. Two nights in a king-size bed with no interruptions: Still paying. Worth every penny.

Shattered

Sometimes when it's quiet, and you're sitting there tuned into the cosmos, you are startled by the sound of sensitive organisms smacking into something hard and inflexible.

Bonk. Ouch. It's the noise made by bunches of gals smacking into the glass ceiling. Over and over; in public life; in corporate life; in all segments of society where women should be and could be running half the show, but aren't.

If it's not the glass ceiling, it's what some women call the sticky floor. Or the concrete wall. Whatever it is, you have to ask: what's the reason for this persistent problem? Why is one-half of our population, better-educated and more qualified than ever, still barely represented in positions of leadership and power?

Not only has the United States never had a woman as president or vice-president, but we rank 60th in the world — behind Andorra — in numbers of women elected to national government, out of over 180 countries that vote. Five states, including Vermont, have never sent a woman to Congress.

In corporate life, a mere 13 percent of corporate directors in Fortune 500 companies are women. Fifty-four of the five hundred have no women directors at all. In 2002, only fourteen of these companies were headed by women. A scant 3.9 percent of these companies' top earners were women.

In education, there are almost three times more men in tenured positions than there are women. Women's tenure rates increased by 1.5 percent over twenty years, compared with an 8 percent increase for men, who were already far ahead in numbers. Most tenured women hold lower ranking jobs than tenured men.

Since the wild and crazy days of women's lib and the Civil Rights Act of 1964, which took a stab at making gender-based discrimination illegal, it seems to a lot of us that our move toward equality has screeched to a dead halt.

A lot of people, of course, blame women for giving up the fight. Sure, a lot of gals who fought for equal rights at work and in public office have stopped agitating, and hustled off to do the jobs they worked so hard to acquire in the first place. They talked the talk; now they're walking the walk.

Meanwhile, they are also doing the society-building chores in family and community that seem to be our provenance. And, the closer you get to women who are the busiest, the louder the bonking sound becomes. As much as they are doing, they are mostly still all working for The Man.

Some people think that our involvement in the care of our families and communities is the reason for the glass ceiling. The traditional argument from executive headquarters is: how can she rise to the top if she can't devote ninety hours a week to work? And the double standard exists: A man who leaves work early for family obligations is a capable, caring mensch. A woman who does the same thing is a disorganized flibbertigibbet with her priorities all wrong.

Is this difference in priorities inborn? Famous women's doctor Christiane Northrup says our fertility-age hormones are the glue that sticks us into caring about our relations as much as we do our jobs. It's our chemistry that make us skip late-night meetings when there's a situation at home.

This sounds like a rerun of the old biology-is-destiny argument that we thought we'd buried years ago. And it's still wrong.

The only reason women rush off to deal with family problems is that nobody else will. And that's still OK with everybody!

For example: the reason that women aren't advancing in academia, according to a 2003 Advancing Women In Leadership report, is that the structure of academics is "based on male career patterns only, and women are not taken into consideration... and it is women who must learn how to cope and succeed in the prevailing system." Bonk! Ow!

Who put that glass ceiling there? Not us.

Don't say there's no better way. In *Madame President*, her book about the ultimate glass ceiling, Eleanor Clift says that when women run congressional committees, there aren't any late-night meetings. And everyone's happy about that, even the men.

A local political expert – a man – told me recently that when women participate in legislation, the result is "more reflective of how we really live." This same expert told me, wistfully, that he'd loved to have taken his 12-week paternity leave when his son was born, but doing so would have had "negative consequences" for his job.

The high-level politician he works for is, of course, a man.

In her book *Sex and Power*, Susan Estrich says, "If more fathers would father more, not only could women mother less, but parenting would be valued more."

The only way to a more balanced view – to keeping concerns of family and community, like child care, education, and health care (what men call 'soft' issues) on an even par with commerce and war – is to get significant numbers of women calling the shots.

The bad news is that guys don't want this to happen. Study after study shows that men invariably, instinctively, help each other to advance while invariably, instinctively, putting barriers in the way of women. Bonk. Ouch.

The good news is that when confronted with this behavior by groups of women, they start to shift. A little. Inch by inch. But it happens. How many women does it take? The magic number isn't a hundred, or ten, but – three.

Three women coming together, reaching up, and giving a little push.

Three women under one roof is all it takes to crack the glass ceiling.

Speak, Mammary:
The Breast Interview

We like to stay informed on the issues, so we had a conversation with a couple of experts in the forefront with whom we've been connected for a while.

Q:What names do you prefer to be called?
RIGHTIE: She's Adorable and I'm Precious.
LEFTIE: We have lots of nicknames. My favorite is "The Big Girls."

Q: Are you breast-cancer activists?
RIGHTIE: No! We are anti-breast-cancer activists. We are against anyone getting breast cancer.
LEFTIE: We decided it was time tell it from our point of view.

Q: Can you tell us your age and experience?
RIGHTIE: We've been around for fifty years or so.
LEFTIE: We're actually not as round as we used to be.
RIGHTIE: We're twins. Not identical.
LEFTIE: I'm bigger.
RIGHTIE: That's normal, so quit bragging.

Q:What made you come out as activists?
RIGHTIE: We were sticking out anyway.
LEFTIE: We noticed that some of our friends weren't doing too well. We felt terrible about that.
RIGHTIE: It made us all sore and achy. We needed to talk to somebody.
LEFTIE: We felt that none of us was getting enough exposure.

Q: So you've felt repressed?
LEFTIE: It's the story of our lives. We've been stuck in bikini tops from the time we were three years old and flat as flapjacks.
RIGHTIE: You try living your life without fresh air or sunshine. No wonder a lot of us aren't feeling so well.

LEFTIE: We weren't made to live like this.

RIGHTIE: We are suffering from terrible restrictions on our freedom.

Q: Are you saying that there are socio-political issues affecting you?

RIGHTIE: We are banned everywhere, except Hooters and National Geographic. We're taboo.

LEFTIE: It's like everyone's forgotten what we are really like. It's so unfair.

RIGHTIE: We may be soft and sensitive, but we still love to go places and do things.

LEFTIE: In our day we were quite a handful.

RIGHTIE: The only things you hear about us these days is controversy or bad news.

LEFTIE: People hear "breast" and think "cancer."

RIGHTIE: Or "implants."

Q: What about "breastfeeding"?

RIGHTIE: Oh, sure, you read about it when somebody is caught nursing in public.

LEFTIE: And then what happens? She gets busted.

Q: So you feel it's an image thing?

LEFTIE: Absolutely. People thinks of us the wrong way.

RIGHTIE: The textbooks call us "secondary sex characteristics."

LEFTIE: We're not secondary anything! We're primary nurturing characteristics.

Q: And you think it's time to restore your reputation.

RIGHTIE: Yes. We are tired of being the problem glands.

LEFTIE: The minute we appear, we are hassled — if we are too big, or too small, or if we jiggle around too much.

RIGHTIE: We can't help it. That's the way we're built.

LEFTIE: Somebody's always worried about seeing too much of us.

RIGHTIE: As if we are a menace to society. When it's really the other way around.

Q: Society is a menace to breasts?

RIGHTIE: Well, we get more health problems here than in most places on the planet.

LEFTIE: Other body parts don't worry about cancer till they're over 50, but not us.

RIGHTIE: It's stressful, always being rated X.

LEFTIE: Everyone knows that stress weakens the immune system.

RIGHTIE: Plus there's the pesticides, the herbicides, the toxic waste, the automobile exhaust.

LEFTIE: Like a certain someone driving us to our mammogram in her gas-sucking SUV.

RIGHTIE: What a boob!

LEFTIE: Not to mention the hormones in the food chain, the Pill, all that estrogen. We're taking it right in the chest.

Q: How would you change things?

LEFTIE: I'd let girls run around top-free from Day One.

RIGHTIE: A little support during exercise, perhaps.

LEFTIE: Treat us nice. Stop thinking of us as obscene.

RIGHTIE: War is obscene. Toxic chemicals are obscene. Anatomy isn't obscene.

LEFTIE: Clean up the air, the soils, the drinking water. How much plastic can one species possibly need?

RIGHTIE: We don't like being treating as premalignant lesions. We're not the problem. Breasts don't cause breast disease any more than lungs cause lung disease.

LEFTIE: We need to be in a breast-friendly culture, or there aren't going to be any of us left.

Q: What do you do to stay in such marvelous shape?

RIGHTIE: We go out, get plenty of sun, exercise, go dancing.

LEFTIE: We love swimming, and baths, and massages.

RIGHTIE: Lots and lots of massages.

LEFTIE: We wish someone would massage us all day.

RIGHTIE: Basically we try to have as much fun as possible.

LEFTIE: We even got a tattoo.

RIGHTIE: Not my idea of fun.

Q: Do you enjoy this kind of publicity?

LEFTIE: We love it. Maybe we'll run for office.

RIGHTIE: We're pretty popular, with both the right and the left. And we love having our picture taken.

LEFTIE: Digital especially – it takes no time to develop.

RIGHTIE: There should be more of us running. We could really perk up a campaign.

Q: What are your future plans?

LEFTIE: We'd like to work for Howard Dean. He has those nice doctor hands.

RIGHTIE: We'd also look pretty good in the Oval Office.

LEFTIE: Or maybe we'll move to Namibia, or the south of France.

RIGHTIE: Where we don't have to wear anything but suntan oil and pearl necklaces.

LEFTIE: And just hang with our friends.

Motherhood in Paradise

Every day, she walked the mile-long beach. Not like the visitors, wandering barefoot in and out of the water before going back to lounge around the pool in our swimwear. She wore sturdy white shoes, a white cap with a brim over a white bandana, dark shades against the dazzling Caribbean sun, and a fresh white shirt. Work clothes.

She carried about forty pounds of merchandise, in a big shoulder bag and on plastic hangers draped over her arms. T-shirts and tank tops, bearing the name of the island or the local beer, folded neatly and stacked in plastic shopping bags. A small case of jewelry made from shells and beads. Bright scarves and wraps – the sarongs that we all wore when we went from our lounge chairs to the bar for a round of coconut crushes for the kids, or a couple of Cuba Libres for ourselves. All her wares were neat and clean, and tidily arranged.

She lugs this paraphernalia, along with her cell phone, drinking water, and a few personal items, up and down the beach, selling at the three vacation spots along the way, every day for the six months or so of the active tourist season. She rarely takes a day off during that time.

I got to know her, as women get to know each other, through our children. I was in the pool with mine and everyone else's, organizing them into swimming and jumping and breath-holding activities, so they'd get to know each other and quit pestering me, so I could do what I like to do in a warm beachy climate, which is read, snooze, swim, and write in my notebooks. The kids, all white, from colder climates, only needed a little encouragement and a few introductions to get it going.

As I was getting out, someone touched my arm. "I want to be in," she grinned – a trim, athletic-looking little gal in a Nike racing suit with her hair in neat cornrows. Dazzling white teeth, black satin skin. "OK," I said. "What's your name?"

Luly, thirteen, spoke American English, and joined in easily as kids do, so it took me a while to figure out that she wasn't a hotel guest, though she was on school break like everyone else. At the end of the day Luly pointed to the woman in white, waiting by the gate.

"That's my mom," Luly said. Beach vendors weren't allowed on the grounds; hotel rules.

Luly herself, as the daughter of a beach vendor, wasn't supposed to be at the pool, but the Antiguan staff let her be. As a non-guest, Luly couldn't get a cold drink at the bar, or lunch from the grill, but the staff loaded my tray with all the provisions I could carry, for whoever I wanted to feed. Luly sat in the shade of an umbrella, blending in like one of the little half-wild cats who crept up for a bit of hot dog or chicken. She and the other children sneaked bits of food to these little creatures, though they weren't supposed to. Hotel rules.

I saw her mother, Aurora, at an umbrella table on the beach one blistering day, not looking too well. I got her something to drink. She told me the security guard, a Jamaican man, was coming down on her for sitting too long, so I got him a drink, too.

She sat for a long time. Her skin is very dark, but I found myself thinking she looked pale. She asked, softly, "Could you get me something to eat?" in accents much more Antiguan than her daughter's. I noticed that she had a broken front tooth, and that the wisps of hair under her bandana were silvery gray, like mine.

The barbecue chef gave me a package to go, and I carried it to her. Her respirations seemed regular; her hands, touching mine, were cool. I didn't check her pulse. I couldn't tell what was going on – there was such a huge amount of information I couldn't get. What I knew for sure was that she was a fifty-something year-old woman, physically exhausted, in a precarious economic situation.

She wouldn't stay to lunch, as she feared consequences from security. She packed up, and walked down the beach where she could sit with friends. She asked if I would be there tomorrow.

Every day, I saw Luly at the pool, and made sure that she, along with the other kids, had lunch, drinks, and the lovely thin sandwiches that the Antiguan staff made for English tea. Every day, I saw Aurora outside the gate; I smuggled food and drink, bribed the guard, and bought some token merchandise, as conducting a sale allowed her more sitting time.

As we sat, she talked – nervously, at first, as the gap between us was as weird for her as it was for me. But it got to be funny. "I'll see you tomorrow, here in my office," she kidded. I liked it when she reminded me, "Get Luly something too, will you?" I said, "Yaah," as in, what do you think I am, a dope? She laughed. We were loosening up.

My departure time loomed. "You could bring me the toiletries from your room. Maybe you could send Luly someting fa school." She was tense and quiet, trying not to sound desperate.

We exchanged addresses and phone numbers. I wondered, Could I do this? Walk the beach every day, not getting past the gates even to check my kid? What if my survival depended upon strangers; on constantly watching, pressing, begging for the least advantage for myself, for my child? I think it would make me sick.

I wondered what would become of Luly if something happened to Aurora. I wonder if she would call me.

That Clinking, Clanking Sound

Wal-Mart is the largest retailer in the world.

The parking lot is always full. A lot of us are going there. Spending. Buying. The company has 6,000 stores and sells more goods than any other chain. Ka-ching.

I know people who don't shop at Filene's, J.C. Penney, or the malls because of the snob factor at those places. Not at the Wall. The help – the associates – are generally a positive, friendly bunch. The only person who ever snubbed me was a gal in Human Resources who wouldn't tell me what associates earn – or even give me a range of wages – when I called to ask.

Maybe the numbers were too bad to say out loud over the phone. The company reports that its *average* full-time hourly wage – nationally – is $9.68 per hour, and that "the majority"– which means over fifty percent – of hourly store associates work full-time, compared to 20 to 40 percent in the rest of retail. Nine dollars per hour, forty hours per week, provides a pre-tax income of $18,000. Family health coverage for employees starts at $155 per month, whittling the gross down to just over $16,000.

The U. S. government's poverty line for a family of four is $18,000.

Wal-Mart typically hires retired workers, part-time employees, students, and people looking for a second income. One business analyst said, "None of them was forced to work at Wal-Mart. If they're working there, presumably that was the best job they could get. If Wal-Mart ceased to exist tomorrow, those people wouldn't be better off."

Wal-Mart workers in China make less than $3 per day. In Bangladesh, they make 13 to 17 cents per hour. These sweatshop workers are, of course, mostly women.

Still, the company reports: "More than half of our associates own company stock through our associate purchase plan." The money flows one way: to the top. Ka-ching.

According to Liz Featherstone, writing for *The Nation*, the company spends millions on right-wing, anti-tax, pro-business, anti-regulatory activities – but, in a recent year, only contributed $6000 to a fund called Wal-Mart Associates In Need. Featherstone writes that education is a priority for the company's multi-billion-dollar foundation (a major tax dodge), but its largesse goes to "mind-numbing and cultish" groups such as Knowledge is Power (KIPP) schools and curricula, which promote regimented rote learning over creative and critical thinking – and are targeted to low-income areas. Critics say that these schools' disciplinary approach, and their reliance on "chanting meaningless slogans" mirrors Wal-Mart's corporate culture. One KIPP teacher told Featherstone, "We're getting them ready for business."

The company's standard practice is to avoid paying taxes – negotiating property tax subsidies for bringing stores to communities that are desperate for business. The Good Jobs First coalition estimates that Wal-Mart has avoided $1 billion in property taxes. That figure doesn't include other taxpayer welfare that the company takes advantage of – Medicaid, food stamps and assistance programs that many employees rely on to subsidize their scanty wages.

Wal-Mart money defies gravity! It only flows up.

Wal-Mart is battling numerous employee rights lawsuits. The biggest is *Betty Dukes v. Wal-Mart Stores,* a sex-discrimination class action representing 1.6 million women. Martha Burk, director of the Corporate Accountability Project, wrote in *Ms.* that women are "at the bottom of the Wal-Mart barrel" concerning wages and promotion. The company's top executives are "all male, all white, all middle-aged, and all sporting the same hairstyle and suit."

The company is the nation's biggest private employer – 1.5 million workers. It is famously anti-union. The *New York Times* describes its tactics as "hardball" and "bare-knuckled." The National Labor Relations Board has filed dozens of complaints against Wal-Mart for tactics such as firing union supporters and withholding bonuses to management if workers unionized. In 2005, when workers at a Canadian store voted to unionize, the company shut the store down. When Wal-Mart meatcutters in Texas voted to form a union in 2000, the company eliminated all of its meat-cutter jobs companywide.

The company is now taking cost-saving steps toward sustainability. A new store in Texas is designed with renewable energy technology: solar arrays, wind turbines, a bio-fuel boiler for burning recovered oil from store operations – an industry first for big box retailers. Savings for Wal-Mart could spur development of alternative-energy technology from marginal resources into industry standards.

The company reports that it is "working on sustainable packaging, cotton, wood, fish, produce, electronics, and the elimination of substances of concern in all merchandise." Sell-out consumer response to an organic-cotton clothing line prompted the company to expand the line. Ka-ching.

According to the U.S. Census Bureau, 37 million people in the U.S. lived in poverty in 2004. Millions more are on the edge as wages stagnate, companies downsize, and basic costs rise. The Libertarian Cato Institute estimates that consumers "save" billions each year because of Wal-Mart's low prices.

Keep wages low for a lot of people. Sell lots of stuff to people with low wages. Sequester your billions at the top. It makes the world go round.

Oh Happy Day

Every so often you get a day that turns out terrific no matter what happens.

It was one of those from the moment I got up. A beautiful cloudless sky. Leftover steak for breakfast. All family members cracking jokes while leaving the house. After a pleasant morning at my desk, I went down to Church Street to register voters. I'd often wondered what it would be like to manage a cart or kiosk on the street, and I think, for one afternoon, I had the best of it. Fine fall weather, good company, the fun of being out there amid the stream of personalities going by; and a little civic action as well.

Administering the Voter's Oath to new Vermont voters is a happy ritual. I'd stand, and read them the promise about casting their vote as they would judge best for the good of the state. Folks would automatically raise their right hands and affirm the oath: "I do." "I will." It's like performing a mini-wedding, right there in public, giving people the power to participate in this democracy. Good vibrations.

With a thick pile of voter registrations filed away at the end of my shift, I went to retrieve to my car, stopping in a nearby coffee shop. Perhaps I was giddy from the whole experience; perhaps it was nostalgia; I don't know what I was thinking, but I ordered a huge cup of dark coffee – the kind I used to live on, in my remote past life. I paid, put on my gloves, and carried the cup to my car. It was a bit after five.

A half-hour later, I was still in my car, crawling up Main Street, sitting through every other green light, gridlocked. No worries. Nice warm drink, music on, plenty of sidewalkers to gaze at. It's all good.

By the time I made it over the top of the hill to my turn onto Spear, my cup was nearly empty, the traffic had normalized, and yessss! I was headed home to cook dinner for my family.

Just past the university athletic complex, a driver in front of me stopped, trying to turn left against a steady rush of oncoming traffic. No problem. I decided to go around her, as there wasn't a break in sight and I was already behind schedule after the creep up Main Street. I carefully edged around her vehicle, and continued on my way, chugging the last of the coffee.

That was when the flashing lights and the blip of a siren went on, right behind me.

A young University of Vermont officer approached, identified himself, and asked me if I knew how fast I was going. Ten miles over? It felt like I was crawling. He asked where I was headed, and I explained. Then the drug kicked in.

"I probably shouldn't have had the triple espresso," I giggled. "I hope you aren't checking caffeine levels, because-that's-probably-the-primary-recreational-drug-of-choice-among-people-my-age..." I heard myself babbling like a lunatic, even as I realized what was happening to my central nervous system. I shut up and took deep breaths. I had, on occasion, been a lot more buzzed in my remote past life, but was having trouble remembering how to deal with it.

He grinned. A noncommittal, professional cop grin. He took my license and registration, went back to the cruiser, and got on the radio, no doubt running the standard wing-nut check. Which took long enough for me to realize the other physiologic effect of an overdose of caffeine. On my bladder.

I had not thought that my term as a notary would include my being stuck in my car, jazzed to the gills, waiting for a man half my age to look up my criminal record, while trying not to widdle.

Not the dignified public-service scenario I'd envisioned.

Stay calm, I told myself. Be cool. Policemen are here to protect us from ourselves. Keep breathing.

Kegel. Kegel. Kegel.

Finally, he came back, sorting my paperwork, and noted that my inspection sticker was about to expire. I mentally braced myself, adding up the cost of the fine plus the windshield that needed replacement, while trying to think of a woodsy turnout on the way to Hinesburg where I could pull in for a discreet wee.

By this time I should have been home cooking spaghetti.

He handed me my stuff, smiled the inscrutable cop smile and said, "Let's just call it a verbal warning this time, shall we? Drive home safely."

Partial sense of relief.

The leaves were nearing peak color, all along the way. I made it home just in time, doing five over the speed limit.

Sometimes there's just no stopping the karma of a great day.

Past Medical History

I'm writing this on a fall day with a brilliant blue sky and russet in the hills – a day exactly like the one on which I lost my mental capacity.

It was a motor vehicle accident. Every fall such a day occurs that reminds me – not consciously, but on a cellular level – of that day: something about the light, the leaves, the high movement of clouds.

Someone in a big truck ran a yield sign. I never saw it coming. My memory around that time, and ever since, is full of giant black holes.

It was the fall of '89. I'd just finished my third year of medical school – the hard year: month after month of hospital rotations, with call every third or fourth night, and one day off between rotations. No time for resting, processing, recreation, family, friends, or love. A mini-taste of what residency is like. My cousin, who'd done it a few years before me, said that his third year wiped him out so badly that he came home and slept for a month afterward. I did that, on a visit with my parents in Maine. I was on my way back to Vermont to tell my dean that I needed more time off.

I got it – about a year, along with some firsthand experience in trauma, intensive care, infectious disease, thoracic surgery, and rehab. I don't know if being a patient for so many months has made me a better doctor; I don't practice conventional medicine, because I have lost the ability to reliably retain new information: anterograde amnesia is the clinical term. I do now know the difference between good doctors and bad ones. The bad ones use their authority as an advantage over a person's weakness and incapacity. A couple of them made mistakes that – shall we say – have left permanent scars. Fortunately, in my case, the bad ones were outnumbered.

The good ones not only involved me in my own care, they pushed me to recover. I remember the day my surgeon showed me my own X-rays on the light board. I was in a wheelchair, with tubes and lines dangling, covering one eye to compensate for the double vision I had at the time. After making me read and assess my own films, he had me go over everyone else's in the bin. It was heartening to find my visual memory intact, though I had trouble with the vocabulary. But he was the first person to make it clear that I would go on. It was a generous and healing moment.

I knew I was lucky – especially the day I came out of the head trauma center after an evaluation. I stepped outside, completely disoriented, unable to remember where in the city I was, or where I'd parked my car. I didn't care. Some of my fellow bum squashes inside were operating their wheelchairs by mouth. That's what people with head injuries were called on one trauma service I worked – 'bum,' as in bad, 'squash,' as in head. I didn't think that was at all funny at the time. Now I get it.

At another evaluation, one old-school doctor used his fingers to thump my skull like a drum – a maneuver I'd never seen. I asked him about it. "It's something we did in the field," he said. He meant war, where there were no X-rays or CAT scans around. "A fracture makes you sound like a cracked pot."

Another one for the funny file.

Many people say that going through trauma or illness can be an exhilarating, liberating experience that rekindles one's joy in living. For me, that's been true. Immediately after the crash, despite double vision, intense pain, and no recollection of what happened five minutes ago, I was euphoric, moved to tears by the taste of an orange, the sight of a bird landing on a twig, or the sound of a voice over the phone. This still happens.

"Emotionally labile" is the clinical term.

"I think your personality has improved," was how one of my colleagues put it.

Love of the art notwithstanding, many people have suggested that it was good I got out of managed care when I did. I didn't have to go through residency, or wear a beeper, or count the number of hours of sleep I was able to get during a night on call.

I traded some percentage of my mental capacity for the privilege of standard REM sleep cycles.

A thoracic surgeon I saw for follow-up surprised me by asking if my accident resulted from sleep deprivation. "We lose one or two residents per year that way," he said. "It's a problem."

Medical training is still run on the old military model, which a U.S. Marine friend once described as identical with the methods of a cult: isolate, indoctrinate, deprive. In 1984, a young woman, Libby Zion, died in a New York hospital due to a mistake by an overworked, sleep-deprived resident, prompting the Bell Commission to limit residents' hours to 80 per week (down from 120). That was twenty years ago. There has been massive resistance to this effort. A Fletcher Allen department head I spoke with recently was still complaining that the 80-hour week limited the work and the 'learning' that residents could achieve. Yet there has been no move to hire more residents (instead of buying more MRIs or adding another wing); or to increase the length of time – five years, say, instead of three – that it would take to complete a residency, if the hours were humanized.

Training systems that require outrageous hours, or 'commitment,' appear to do this to preserve the old model that was created by and for men without families, or with traditional wives: the old model that excluded women except as unpaid, ancillary labor. Excluding women excludes change. In the twenty years since the death of Libby Zion, there has been essentially no change in the way doctors are trained. Isolate. Indoctrinate. Deprive.

In the locker room at the gym the other day, I met a woman, a respected teacher, a professor, a dean at the medical school; a woman who embodies compassion and clarity, and who helped me get back on track. I congratulated her on her retirement, and expressed dismay that the changes we were so hopeful of back in the 1980s – in medical education, in gender equity, in patient-centeredness, in reverence for the environment – had not arrived; had, in fact, at Fletcher Allen Health Care and the College of Medicine, been reversed, eroded.

She told me that there are now only two women left in the administration of the College of Medicine. She said, "It is not a healthy place to be a woman." Then, "Ours is not a benign profession."

I do remember what the opposite of "benign" is. It is not a good diagnosis.

I'm thinking, on this bittersweet day, of the women in our profession – now at least half of all physicians in training – who are entering a milieu that is not truly designed with their, or anyone's, well-being in mind. It doesn't take a rocket scientist to figure out why so many women and children are not having our needs met under the present system.

I regret that I've been unable to change things.

Cheers, Friends!

The candles are lighted; it's holiday time,
And, wassail in hand, I'm in search of a rhyme.
My editor gives me an 800-word parameter,
So unlike Moore and Seuss, I can't stick to anapestic tetrameter.
Still, I'll begin at the top of my list,
And wish the best wishes that ever were wished
To all Vermont women, and the men we are next to,
And everyone transgendered and intersexed, too.

Here's to the presses! Hail and hosanna!
The St. Albans Messenger, the Bennington Banner,
Out In The Mountains, and the Brattleboro Reformer,
May all your solstices be brighter and warmer!
To the Free Press, with Susans Reid and Allen,
And to Mike Donoghue, champagne by the gallon.
And sparkles of glitter, and tidings of joy,
To Geoff and all the Gevalts – oy!
Cheers, Times-Argus! You took the prize.
Cheers, Seven Days! You keep us street-wise.
I wish a season full of mirth
To Peter Freyne and Peter Kurth,
And a round of huzzas, please,
For Jernigan Pontiac and Rusty Dewees –
Columnists who make my days seem brighter,
(And my writing, I hope, a little bit tighter).

Bring in the dancers! The artists! The bards!
Woody Jackson's cows to stand in our yards.
Season's blessings upon dear Dug Nap,
Felicia Darling, Elisabeth von Trapp,
To April St. Francis, Bonnie Mennell,
Judy Alexander, Big Joe Burrell,
Senator Pat Leahy, and Marcelle.
And peace and love, and shining light

To our State Senators – Claire Ayer to Jeanette White,
Serving Vermonters from border to border;
And State Reps Zuckerman to Adams, in
Reverse alphabetical order.
Let's sing a chorus of praises and hymns
for Douglas and Jeffords, our two Jims.

To the political parties, from the left to the right,
We'd like to wish a nice long Silent Night.

Cheers to the crews at the mill and the mall!
And the Vermont Youth Orchestra, back from Carnegie Hall.
And to everyone in our seats of knowledge,
Like Elizabeth Coleman at Bennington College.
And, while we are busily hitting the books,
A toast to Chris Bohjalian, and Tim Brookes;
To Eugenie Doyle – a clap and a stomp –
Grace Paley, Reeve Lindbergh, and Billy Romp,
Howard Frank Mosher, Alexia Brue,
Julia Alvarez, and the Gihon River Review.

Here's a magnificent wreath of holly
For Bill Lippert and Diane Carmolli;
And Peter Clavelle – is he still mayor?
And Norwich Cadet Colleen Thayer.
Jingle bells rockin' around the clock
For Mark Phillippe and Julia Brock,
Cheryl Gibson, Nan Reid, Peggy Cohen,
Judy Luce, Laura Mann, Josie Cronin,
And those who work from dark to dawn
To keep women healthy, and get babies born.

If I need to get the party flyin'
I'll ask Jay Craven, and John O'Brien,
And bring in a dose of docu-drama
With filmmaker Anjalika Sharma.
And if it's not considered excessively jocky,
I'll bring in the CVU Girls' Soccer team, and Hartford Field Hockey!
Cris Ericson would make the evening hot,

Although there's still no legal pot
(Vermont's Marijuana Party would clearly gain
By moving to the State of Maine).

Days of joy and nights of peace
to Melinda Estes and Melissa Deas.
Choirs of angels will certainly chant
For Evelyn Kwanza and Wanda Heading-Grant,
And all the others who've made music for us,
Like the Community Choir, and South County Chorus.
Bring up the lights and strike up the band
For the Snelling gals, Barbara and Diane;
For Beth Robinson and Ruth Uphold,
And the Champlain ferry pilots, steaming through the cold.
And then a round of precious treats
For the snowplow drivers who clear our streets.

I'd have Maura O'Sullivan make a great dinner
For Jodi Williams, our own Nobel Prize winner,
And there'd be a plum pudding to stick a spoon in,
Set aflame for our ex-Governor, Madeleine Kunin.
I'd keep plenty of sweet things bakin'
For Alison Bechdel and Lola Aiken,
Jean Ankeney, Diana "Spy" Barnard,
and the men and women of the Vermont National Guard.

And give a special holiday wish
To the artists formerly known as Phish;
We're glad you gave us Coventry.
Does Casey Rea agree with me?

O, alas! Though I feel I'm just starting to warm up
I'm afraid that I've used the allowable form up.
So, be blessed, and merry! Please don't drink and drive!
And may peace and joy be with us all in '05.

PART THREE

Dr. Trixie's Prescriptions

Baggage

I love it when it's warm enough to drive around with the windows open, with all the signs of spring bursting forth. Ancient cemetery lilacs in bloom; new foals and calves in the herds; red-wing blackbirds staking out turf on fence posts and cat-tail stalks.

The fields are freshly plowed, losing their winter stubble; others are waiting to dry. In the lowest, wettest pasture on the road to the elementary school, I saw a white speck on the ground, far off the road, between two puddled rows of cut stalks. An errant snow goose? A white cat out hunting? Around here there's always some nature exhibit giving free lessons.

It was actually a plastic shopping bag. Far enough out of reach, so that someone would have to pull on mud boots, slog through heavy clay and puddles, and slog back – about twenty minutes' worth of counter-litterbug activity. It stayed there for two weeks, before finally getting plowed under. A tag end still sticks out of the new furrow.

A couple of days a week, while waiting at the end of the driveway for the kindergarten bus, I pick up a diet soda bottle or a beer can or a cigarette pack that some low-lifer has chucked out the window into the ditch. I spot plastic bags and wrappers on the side of the road, along stream banks, and in the turnouts where I pull in to answer my cell. It's not as bad as places I've seen, like the Dominican Republic, where the hurricane winds whip litter into the tall trees, and leave it festooning the beach like some bizarre seaweed. I read somewhere that in South Africa there are so many plastic bags littering the landscape that citizens have nicknamed them "the national flower."

Every so often, on the road to town, there's the entire black garbage bag of unmentionables that has flown intact and unnoticed out the back of somebody's pickup truck.

At the grocery store, when asked "Paper or plastic?" I say, "Fabric," and hand over my collection of cloth totes – an idea I stole from a woman in front of me at the register one day. In one of the totes, I keep a few small produce and bread bags to reuse, all organized for grab and go, in my cubby in the mud room.

Still, the bags pile up. The guy of the house won't go the tote-bag route. It's not spontaneous enough, or else he likes the aesthetic of fresh plastic grocery bags nestled among the tool boxes in the back of his truck.

And – I blush to admit this – there is also the mall problem. A new bag per person per trip, minimum. So in they creep.

A few go into the glove box for auto trash. A bunch more line wastebaskets in the bathroom and bedrooms. Fresh clean ones end up as packing material, which I realize is a sleazy way of foisting the problem onto somebody in, say, Bangor, or Beverly Hills, where perhaps they won't notice. The rest end up in the 'bag bag' in the pantry, where they undergo exponential replication until we can't shut the door any more. Then I ball up an armful of the oldest, gummiest ones, and throw them away – into the kitchen trash, which I have lined with 13-gallon bio-degradables from the EcoStore. Who are we kidding? What a civilization, buying things for no other purpose than to throw them away.

I would love to line the trash bin with them, but they don't fit the one we've had for 20 years. I could buy a smaller one, but then what would I do with the old one? Put it in a garbage bag and throw it away?

I once tried to recycle a whole bunch of IGA bags back at the IGA. The cashier gave me the kind of look reserved for the criminally insane, and jammed them into the trash.

On a visit to the American Folk Art Museum in New York, I saw a lovely rug crocheted entirely out of Wonder Bread bags, nicely framed and lighted. There's an idea. Maybe I could braid up some bath mats.

We Americans throw away 100 billion plastic bags each year. And that is just the tip of the iceberg.

My accumulation of styrofoam trays goes to the school art department, who'll take everything I have. I don't even want to think about styrofoam peanuts (known in the trade as "angel poop"). I've stopped ordering from companies that use them, including my favorite discount book supplier in Connecticut. I had been recycling them to a local potter, who used them in shipping his wares, but the last time I took over a batch, he pointed to his 30-foot storage silo and said, "Sorry – we're full."

Other, more sensible nations have instituted a tax of ten to twenty cents per plastic bag acquired in stores. In Ireland, for example, a seventeen-cent tax reduced bag use by around 90 percent. American chains push plastic, as the bags are about half the price of paper; a rise in oil prices may change that. Maybe by then we'll be all bagged out.

The Cure

⚊⚊

Back by popular demand – Dr. Trixie's prescription for all-natural hormone replacement therepy.

So – we are all worried that we can't take estrogen any more. Who needs it? Pills made of pipi from pregnant horses? Who thought this was a good idea? Estrogen makes you bloated, sore-breasted, and eager to eat everything in sight. It makes you feel like you're pregnant. It gives you cancer. Is this what we really want in the bloom of our maturity?

Guys like to get women on estrogen 'cause it makes us docile and placid. No mood swings, no bitching, no hot flashes of truth. All those perfectly normal things they think of as symptoms.

But it's not the estrogens we miss in the 'Pause. It's the *androgens*. It's a scientific fact that young ovaries produce lots and lots of androgens. That's the feelgood stuff. That's what makes you strong, brave, aggressive, and eager to stay up all night doing the wild thing. It's the decline in androgens that makes you blue and weepy, like you don't care if you ever go shopping or have another orgasm again.

That's bad. That's a problem.

There is a cure. Don't bother your doctor, don't start injectables; they'll cost a lot of money and give you zits. The formula we need is free, natural, and readily available; in fact, there's presently an oversupply in this country.

You know what I'm talking about: that little twig and berries arrangement down in the undies of the guy who's snoring away in your bed. Some people call 'em Big Dogs, but like a lot of marketing, that can be misleading.

If you are a lesbian, it's not a problem. Surely you have friends who would help out like they did when you wanted a kid.

Eeew, you say. You have spent your entire life avoiding the dreaded blow job.

What kind of attitude is that? Look at the positives. With most guys it takes about two minutes. A couple of beers beforehand can make it even quicker.

Of course, Viagra may throw that off somewhat. But twice a week, two minutes, is nothing when you start to appreciate the benefits. Your mental focus improves. Your skin becomes stronger and more elastic – especially those little lines around your mouth. How do you think those old gay guys get those killer complexions?

For you blondes out there, yes, you do have to swallow.

Any iron-pumping gym rat will tell you that it's androgens that beef up your muscle tone, strength, and coordination. See Jane pop that pickle jar open, muscle the trash cans onto the back of the truck, and drag that Lawn Boy out of the ditch with her bare hands.

There are additional benefits too, which you may notice right away. The house is vacuumed, the oil is changed in your car, the recyclables are out the door on time, and you are not lifting a finger.

In medicine we call this the donor effect.

He's starting to arrange quality time for the two of you. Private moments. Sexy little dates. Go figure. With me, he brings a tea tray into the bedroom in the morning, and gets the kids off to school early, saying "I'll be right back! WAIT HERE!"

I have a new bookshelf in the study. My tires are rotated. The bathroom floor is buffed to a deep gloss. You see where I'm going here. This could change the world.

Drug precaution: If you start swilling tallboys, subscribing to the hockey channel, and leaving the seat up, you should probably to cut back your dose.

And — for further investigation: you've heard about male menopause. Andropause. The new disease the medical establishment thought up to create a midlife-crisis hormone market for men. Guys who are worried about this now have a whole new option to consider.

That would really change the world.

Let Them Eat Wedding Cake

I laugh when I hear about anybody – gay, lesbian, whatever – clamoring to get married. What can they possibly be thinking?

Sure, you want to get hitched. Tie the knot. Put on the battleship chains. Get all dolled up in tuxes and beaded satin and have your picture in the paper. Do you know what you are letting yourself in for?

Hetero marriage statistics – the only kind we have so far – show that while half the population is rushing to pick out china, the other half is storming off to Splitsville, clogging up the family courts with huge lists of grievances and nasty property disputes.

Over 50 percent of first marriages end in divorce. For second marriages, it's over 30 percent. And then there's Elizabeth Taylor. One hundred percent. You'd think the peculiar institution of marriage would be the last thing anyone would want to borrow from the straights.

Back in the Dark Ages, Anglo-European marriage laws evolved as a way of keeping property in the hands of men. As women couldn't own real estate, the property under consideration was the woman herself, who was known as chattel. As were children. Any babes born to a marriage were considered legal offspring belonging to the husband.

On paper this sounds like a fun deal for everyone involved. A man could beget children with a married woman, and they'd be taken care of by the lord of the manor. A married woman could produce children by whomever she fancied, and they'd count as her husband's. No wonder the errant knights and ladies of yore spend so much time galloping around between castles.

Then Henry The Eighth came along, legalized divorce, and wrecked the whole system.

Sure, marriage comes with tax breaks, company benefits, community property, and next-of-kin status. But what if one of you has a bunch of assets, and the other one goes way far down the black hole of bankruptcy? Are you still in there for better or worse? Oh, sure, you can get a pre-nup. The purpose of a pre-nup is to assure the courts that what's yours is yours, and will remain that way. Duh! Just like it would if you stayed single!

I overheard someone ask a friend why she wasn't getting hitched to the guy she'd been with for twenty years and four kids. "I prefer being the mistress," she said. "When one of them asks me where their socks are, I say, 'I don't know. Do you see a wife around here anywhere?' That shuts them up."

I wondered about the vocabulary. "If you're the mistress, what's he?"

"The mattress," she grinned. It works for them.

But wait, there's more. Don't tell me you forgot the in-law thing. So your lover's parents are giving you grief now because of your relationship with their offspring. Shake it off! They're not your relatives! But the second you sign that paper in the presence of the JP, every nutball in the family becomes your kith and kin.

This means that they can borrow car payments from your shared finances, hit you up for tuition, drop their behaviorally-challenged kids off for vacations, horn in on your holidays, and suck you into every familial Ponzi scheme that comes along. And! They can pop in to pull this stuff any time, day or night, without calling ahead! They're family!

If you were only living in sin, they'd leave you in peace.

I know. You want your/your partner's children growing up under the security of a two-parent regime. I admit that marriage in this light makes sense, as the appropriate sass-back to "I don't have to mind you! You aren't my mother/father!" thus becomes, "Tell it to a lawyer, pal!"

But so far, it's always women and children who go tumbling down the socioeconomic ladder in divorce. And – take heed – it's never single mothers you hear about losing their children in vile custody battles.

My own dear parents had an agreement that whoever left first had to take the six kids.

Interesting that our POTUS wants to spend our tax money trying to get the poor heteros married off – and nobody else. It's also interesting that most religious and tribal traditions frown on mixed marriages. What could be more mixed, I ask you, than a union between a man and a woman? Negative and positive? North and south? Mars and Venus? As in, What alien left those Speedo briefs drying on the shower head?

Maybe it's hetero marriages, with their abysmal failure rate, their record of rampant domestic violence, and a worse recurrence rate than herpes, that ought to be banned. Maybe it's time for another group of people to show us a new way of doing things.

I wish you joy.

The Bare Necessities

I know some of you have been waiting, so here it is. Dr. Trixie's Guide to Erotic Dance.

This came about when a gentleman I know, in Arts and Entertainment, invited me to a local club, in the interest of Journalism and the Media. Kind of a cross-training affair. I am, after all, concerned with all the working women of Vermont.

I'd never been to a strip club before, but I'd been to one bachelorette party featuring the Chippendales, whose get-'em-up-and-moving dance style was lots of fun, along with their ingenious tear-away costumes, which they shed with exuberance and great choreography. I dutifully tucked tip money into their pouches, whenever one came by.

My learned guide gave me the drill: You go in and chat with the dancers. Then they take turns dancing and taking their clothes off. Despite, or maybe because of, having worked in a lot of women's clinics, I was glad to hear that the artists kept their bottoms on.

I spent about two seconds wondering what to wear. Who cares!

We went in and sat at a table. Several lovely young women came and chatted with us. Told us their club names, which weren't their real ones, though I was pleased that one called herself Trixie.

A girlfriend in L.A. had filled me in on "Stripper Aerobics," an exercise program where participants are encouraged to pick out "Stripper Names." You do this by combining the name of your first pet with the name of the first street you ever lived on. My gentleman friend's would, for example, be "Shuggie Maple." I'm not telling you mine, in case I ever end up having to use it, say, to supplement my fixed income at the Assisted Living facility.

The young women told us little things about themselves – their other jobs; their kids – that may or may not have been true; in this business, I imagine you try to retain what privacy you can. They wore foxy outfits – micro-skirts; bustiers; strappy, clingy dresses; very high heels. Their makeup was pretty – subtle. They looked healthy and buff. They all claimed to be around eighteen.

Each performer had a CD that the doorman played after announcing her name. She then went to a small floor with a bar enclosing it, and started dancing around one of the floor-to-ceiling metal poles installed there. The music included classic AC/DC, some headbanging metal, and the current teenybopper hip-hop favorite, "My Hump," by the Black-Eyed Peas.

The strippers did pullups and spins around the pole for a bit, then moved to a far corner and shucked off their things as if they were going straight into the hamper. No tease, just off. Perhaps that's what the audience likes.

One strong, limber dancer shimmied up the pole, then leaned over backward and slid her dress off upside down, which was, I thought, an excellent move.

After the pole routine, the dancer, top-free, in basic thong and high heels, moved to the bar. My guide explained the Rules. Guys at the bar give money to the dancers, who perch and wiggle and recline in front of each patron till the money stops. The guys may not touch the gals – nowhere, nohow. The gals could touch the guys, but that seemed limited to hands-on-shoulders kind of stuff. A gal could take dollar bills, fold them, tuck them behind a guy's ears, then take them back with her teeth. No kissing.

Or, when a dancer hopped up on the bar, a patron could slip bills under the strap of her thong – if she, not he, lifted the strap off her skin. The women squatting on the bar moved in very, very close. One dancer positioned herself, squatting in her heels and thong, so that her thighs almost touched a patron's ears. The men sat there frozen like game in jacklights.

The dancers were very smooth-looking. Pristine. They must have spent fortunes in body-hair removal and tanning. Subtle tattoos, subtle piercings; nothing outrageous. Tasteful.

Contrary to my expectations, there wasn't even much drinking going on. No rowdies jumping up on chairs hollering "More, more!" and waving fistfuls of cash, like the women did at the Chippendales event. This was restrained. Sedate. A highly regulated culture, like that of the geisha; like Kabuki. Like Noh: No misbehaving, no acting out, no touching, no interactivity, and absolutely no sexual expression. All ritual, all gesture. Everyone observing the Rules.

Almost church-like in a way, except for "My hump-my-hump-my-hump" over and over.

My guide indicated two booths with red velvet curtains, where customers could, for twenty bucks, purchase the complete attention of a dancer for ten or fifteen minutes. There was also a room, wedged between the dance bar and the bathrooms, where, for a hundred bucks, customers may buy more time. The Rules: in the Booth, she may show more, but he still can't touch. In the Room, she may touch; but he must remain fully clothed.

Rather reminiscent of the way we Catholic girls used to keep track of which base we were on, back in the day.

The bar was small; I observed one customer negotiate a Booth session with a dancer. A millisecond of distaste crossed her face before they went behind the curtain. Let's get this over with.

What surprised me were the bills – green flowers that the little dancers fluttered to like exotic butterflies. Not twenties, not tens, not even fives – all ones, which the artists tucked away before fluttering off to the next patron. This seemed like a slow night. Each dancer might get four or five dollars from three or four patrons for each dance. They might dance five or six dances. Maybe they'd get a client into a Booth, or a Room. They worked till one or two in the morning. After paying the club and all their other job-related expenses, I figure that, like a lot of part-time working women, at the end of their shift they weren't raking in a tremendous lot of take-home pay.

Just enough to cover the bare necessities.

Blinded With Science

Harvard President Larry Summers hit the nail on the head. It is part of our cultural mythology that women's biology – which really means our bodies – is the reason for our exclusion from everything you can think of that men have wanted to keep for themselves.

We are made somewhat differently from guys. For this reason we haven't been allowed to go to school, own property, or vote.

Lately it's why we don't go into math and the sciences; or if we do, why we don't succeed in reaching top positions. But as one of a gazillion women trained in science, I am sure that it's not our distinctly-configured bodies, or even our distinctly-configured brains, that are the impediment to our advancement.

Women have about as much chance of advancing in the sciences as they do in, say, the NFL. Or the Vatican. I made a joke about this at a recent alumni meeting at Harvard. I said, "Women in the sciences are required to take vows of poverty, chastity and obedience. Poverty, because we earn 79 cents to every dollar a man earns. Chastity, because you can't get anywhere on the Mommy track. Obedience, because you are never going to be the Pope." None of the women laughed.

The National Football League, the Vatican, and "science" as we know it were all conceived entirely without the input or consideration of you-know-who. The NFL and the Church make no bones about this. Science, on the other hand, claims to be unbiased and objective. It isn't; it is as chauvinist and dogmatic as any religion, and as impervious to cultural critique. If you don't believe as we believe, they say, then you aren't really one of us.

We forged ahead anyway. It was the women's health movement that liberated medicine from its dependence on the 70-kilogram male as its standard for every measure of health – including the hematocrit, a measure of red blood cells. In 1987, the UVM pathology department was still using the hematocrit of the 70-kg male as the normal value. Those of us who'd worked in women's clinics knew from observation and records that women tolerate a lower, wider range of hematocrit – which makes sense, given our bleeding cycles. I pointed this out to the professor, who said, "Well, there haven't been any studies published on this" – never mind the vast amount of information in circulation from the very women's clinics I mentioned. He said, "Our protocol is to treat everyone whose values are below this standard, whether they are symptomatic or not."

A low hematocrit is an indication of anemia, which is treated with iron pills, which, as anyone knows who has taken them, are not without side effects. A lab test book that I later consulted did provide separate hematocrit values for women and men. How could it be in the best interest of an expert in the field not to know this, or care, other than that the facts were irrelevant to his view of medicine?

Examples of this innate bias abound. A chief medical officer at Fletcher Allen Health care, consulted by a woman with a uterine fibroid problem, recommended the standard therapy: hysterectomy. "The uterus is a dumb organ," he said; "All it does is bleed." It is astounding that a person who holds that view would rise to the top in a career in women's reproductive health, and in health care in general; but that's the way it is. And everyone seems OK with that.

At the University of Vermont College of Medicine, out of twenty or so departments (medicine, surgery, obstetrics, etc.) only four have ever been chaired by women; yet women now make up fifty percent or more of each medical school class. In the vast administration of the College, there are still only two senior officers who are women. In graduate schools across the country – in law, in journalism, in the humanities – women outnumber men as students; yet they lag far behind in tenure, in administration, and in the heads of departments.

The reason for this may be biology – but it isn't ours. Women, and men, are capable of mastering calculus and particle physics. Women, and men, are capable of designing Nobel-quality research. Women and men are capable of holding department chairmanships and college presidencies. And women, and men, are capable of shuttling children to play dates, organizing child care, and getting meals on the table. The chief difference between us is that men refuse to take physical and temporal responsibility for the children they engender – because the design and engineering of their 'careers', their reluctance to share turf, and their insistence on low-paid, or unpaid, female servitude, take precedence. But all this is really because they think their biology makes them this way.

Anthropologist Margaret Mead said that in every culture she ever saw, men have staked out spheres of activity from which women are excluded. Science in particular is blind to its own pattern of exclusion. Which is unfortunate, as perhaps the use of scientific methods of analysis and design could help fix the problem.

Changing Hands

A friend told me that her son, whose left arm – his pitching, batting, shooting arm – was broken, and immobilized, went out to the driveway to teach himself to shoot 'righty,' even before he had surgery to fix the break. In two hours, he got pretty consistent. He is fifteen years old.

Changing from a left-handed to a right-handed way of life is a such a huge shift in thinking that it alters brain circuits – it makes the brain redesign itself to accommodate a new way of life, a new skill-set, a different spatial approach to the world. My friend's son did this in less time than it takes to read the Sunday paper.

That made me think about the culture of change.

In medical school, I was in a class on "Problems in Gynecology" with a professor who was covering the problem of PMS. She said, "OK, what are the causes?" The class came up with the usual litany – too much estrogen; not enough progesterone; too much caffeine; not enough sleep. The 'nontraditional' students – older women – in the class just looked at each other. Then we swung into action: The causes of PMS are society's repression of women's monthly cycles; our lack of political representation; the 79 cents to the dollar wage differential; and too much housework. The professor looked at us and said, "But you can't change that. You'd have to change the culture." We said, "Oh yes we can!" And she said, "Then hurry up! Change the culture!"

In medicine, it took us about 100 years to change the habit of using the 70-kilogram male as the physical standard for all of humanity. This change came about through the work of the women's health movement, where the clinics, the procedures, and the data-collecting were all designed with the well-being of women in mind. That experience altered the medical landscape.

The 'problem' of women in science, in journalism, in foreign policy, in Congress, is not a woman problem. It is a culture problem. It is women trying to fit into an environment that's been designed without any of our input, or consideration of our wants, needs, or production schedules.

Take the standard of the 80-hour work week. Women, many of whom who use our brains differently – more broadly, one could argue – than the average man, may not be satisfied with a work schedule that leaves little time for other considerations. It's not that we want less work; it's that we need more of everything else as well – like community time, connectivity with our families and friends, a wider range of brain activity. Maybe we like more balance. You have to look at it for whatever it is, not compare it to the male standard. Instead of always trying to fit in and keep up with the status quo, we should be analyzing the way all these things – the residency program, the newsroom, the Senate, the World Bank – would look like if we designed them, if we had an equitable say in their conception. No doubt they would look quite different.

Of course there are men who are with us on a lot of this. At most places where we work, the guys already talk the talk. But they still don't see the biases of their own culture. Nancy Hawkins, the woman who walked out on Larry Summers' speech about women being biologically disadvantaged in the sciences, spearheaded a study at MIT that looked at the inequities between women and men on the faculty. The men gave each other promotions, corner offices, huge chunks of lab space and hordes of graduate students; the women got endless committee work and longer hours with less pay. When the men in the department were confronted with these data, they said. "This can't be us!" They were shocked at their own behavior. All this time they thought they were being supportive.

Susan Estrich, in her book "Sex and Power," used this story as an example of the ingrained way men have of relating to each other, of thinking of men as "us" and women as "them." She also said that all it takes is three women in such an environment – like Nancy Hawkins and her two colleagues – to come together and alter the milieu.

Advertising mogul Linda Kaplan Thaler said in her book "Bang!" that there is a physical high that comes from cooperative activity. Physiologically, it's the same high that comes from seeing a beautiful picture, or eating chocolate or dessert. She selects her team for this capability; she creates a culture of cooperativity from it. In medicine we see this phenomenon in the response of patients who heal faster when their surgeons take the time to sit on their beds, converse, and make contact; in the lessening of pain in patients in cancer wards, when pets are brought to visit; and in labor and delivery, when mother and baby, if encouraged, and unimpaired by drugs and interventions, cooperate in a pain-lessening exchange of hormones – oxytocin – and endorphins. It's not magic, it's science. Cooperativity makes things go well. It fosters a kind of bliss.

I read somewhere that it takes an amazingly small percentage of a population – 20 percent – to bring about a shift in thought, like being cooperative around race or culture or gender. The vocabulary for such change is already in place.

My friend's southpaw son, teaching himself to shoot and pitch righty in two hours, shows how fast such a change can come about.

Wired

Everything comes by e-mail these days: jokes, letters from family and friends, and a report from my father in Maine that my mother went to her doctor to be seen for a cough, and found out she had a malignant pleural effusion around her right lung. Malignant pleural effusion puts a tumor at Stage 4. That's as far as it goes.

Later, over the phone, when I thanked Dad for his note and got more details, he said, "I e-mailed all of you" – meaning his six kids, coast to coast – "because I didn't know whom to call first." He's always been an equal opportunity kind of guy.

My mother herself e-mailed us the details of the pathology report, and some info from her doctor on the chemotherapy she was proposing to start.

We then e-mailed a list of all our cell phone numbers to each other and to Dad.

He e-mailed us Mom's hospital room phone number, and suggested the best times to call. She hasn't been feeling well enough for visitors, but she enjoys short phone calls, some of which are pretty funny, as:

ME: Mom, I heard you had your head scarves all picked out.

MOM: Actually I just heard about a place in Bangor that provides wigs and cosmetics for women undergoing chemo, so I'm going with that.

ME: So, Mom, tell me – are you gonna go red?

MOM: No way! BLONDE.

The initial round of Taxotere didn't go so well, so she landed back in the hospital with some complications, and decided no more chemo. Palliative care. She's 80 years old. She said, "It's my life – I am doing it my way. And I don't want to see anyone right now."

Dad e-mailed us that she was concentrating very hard on what she has to do, and feared being distracted. He said, "I'll let you know when she's ready."

I sent her a funny card, and set my travel bag out with a few things in it, ready to go.

Dad e-mailed us about the next procedure, to drain the fluid and do an intervention that will prevent its recurring. He also mentioned planning for home nursing care whenever she leaves the hospital.

We siblings e-mail each other highlights of our phone calls with our mother. My youngest sister wrote, "She likes the view from her room." Eastern Maine Medical Center is a beautiful place on the Penobscot River, with green courtyards, and a view of the water from every patient room. Bald eagles fly up the river looking for fish. It's one of the best-designed hospitals I've ever seen.

Still, it's not home. My sister wrote: "Mom said the only thing she felt like eating was the hummus that Dad had made and brought in a jar."

We siblings supplement our e-mails with a lot of phone time, during which a surprising amount of lighthearted humor occurs, as we reminisce and plan and distract each other. Needless to say, some of us aren't getting very much work done.

I was thinking how different the connections were in my mother's younger days – operator-switched phone lines; post offices with mechanical scales; bumpy back roads. My mother said she once drove Route 1 from Augusta, Maine to Boston, and back again, to buy a pair of shoes. It must have taken twelve or fourteen hours, all told. That was it for same-day delivery.

Years later, my mother, who was active in both the sex-education movement and the Girl Scouts, and has always had a wicked sense of humor, brought home a poster that cracked us up. It showed a young woman, quite pretty, and quite pregnant, in a green Scout uniform with pins and sash and badges, with her hands on her humungous belly and a sly look in her eye. The caption was "BE PREPARED."

I was always the last of my peers to get wired: to have an electric typewriter, a computer, Internet access, a cell phone; and I always acquired those things with reluctance. But right now I'm very glad for the elegance of this technology. It's helping me be prepared – for whatever happens next, while I wait for the next signal.

The Watch

My best friend in med school, Dr. Jane — who started out as a home-birth midwife — said that the first two things medical students should learn are labor-sitting, and death sitting.

We were taught neither. Certainly we were never led to believe that sitting down, anywhere, was a good thing. We learned the 'stages' of labor, and of dying, but we never sat with people; we 'rounded on patients.' It was pretty much an in-and-out kind of management style.

One of my classmates actually got busted for offering massage to people on her service. The patients liked it; it was the doctors who objected.

I never got to actually stay with a woman throughout an entire labor, in the hospital. We were taught to pop in and out of the labor rooms for periodic checks, and then go in for the 'delivery.' We rarely had established any previous connection with whoever came in, so to a lot of us, the hospital approach felt like a violation of privacy: "Hi there, I'm the medical student, are you ready to push?" Not the kind of presence you would ideally want in an intimate moment, or at a major life passage.

Nobody is really with you in that setting; they have other things on their minds: the patient in the next room; the end of their shift; utilization review breathing down their necks. This is not to say there aren't moments of grace; but still, the main process going on in any hospital isn't the patients'.

It's much the same with dying. People pop in and out, though at a different pace than in labor and delivery. There are long stretches of being left alone, unless someone other than hospital personnel is attending. For one patient I met, Mr. G, in end-stage heart failure, there was no one.

One of his nurses told me, "Why don't you go in and sit with him?"

I did. They'd given him a quiet room with a beautiful view of birch trees and snow. He was a charming old Italian gentleman, white-haired, very thin and pale. I sat in a chair beside him. He offered his hand, and I took it.

He didn't have the strength to talk much. He flirted a little, to break the ice. He told a few short stories. Mostly we just sat and held hands. Sometimes I checked his pulse or his breathing, but mostly we just sat. It was weird at first, but soon became the highlight, and the focus, of my days.

My resident and my team cut me, I thought, a lot of slack to do that, as I certainly wasn't doing any other work while I sat with Mr. G, over a week or so, holding hands and watching the snow melt as he grew weaker and weaker.

Then, of course, my time was up, and I had to transfer off that service and go to another hospital; it was all about the schedule. Mr. G told me, "When you leave, I'm gonna die."

The day after I left, my resident called me and said, "He died." I imagined his dying according to protocol, with people whisking quietly in and out of the room to check his vitals, and nobody staying to hold his hand.

My mother is spending her final time at home, with my father, her husband of fifty-four years. She's in quite a lot of pain, but she doesn't want to be overly medicated. She wants to be with him, and hold his hand.

They sit for hours together, quietly, or communicating in the minimal way people have who know each other's thoughts. She drifts in and out of a dream state with the narcotics, but it's he with whom she is most lucid, most aware. He attends her round the clock, giving her scheduled meds at ten and twelve p.m., and again at four in the morning, keeping a precise record of the medication and dosage.

I thought this a pretty demanding schedule for an 80-year-old guy, but he said, 'I'm the only one who has nothing else to think about but her." He said, "A nurse would be thinking about her own family. I'm not concentrating on anything but taking care of your mother. There's nowhere else she could get this kind of care."

"She would have done it for me," he said.

We, their children, are gathering to spell him for some of the sitting, attending our mother during this difficult passage, as her breathing becomes labored, and her least movement causes pain; but mostly we are here to take care of the details, the housekeeping, the food supply, the laundry, and the telephone, so that he can sit beside her for as long as they like, holding her hand.

Coming Home

The long drive back from Maine, on Route 2, is something I've done a hundred times. On a bright fall day, with a panorama of changing leaves, and little traffic on the road, it can be a meditative experience. Six hours of meditation, with music and occasional rest stops, isn't the worst way to reflect on the passing of a life.

My young daughter and I listened to Mozart, piano jazz, and silence. She slept a lot, in her car seat, processing the past few weeks in her own ways; I drove, and thought about the life I had left behind, and the one I was heading back into.

An old friend who now lives in L.A. recently spent time in New York, attending the death of her own mother. The day after my mother died, she told me, "It was hard for me to leave. When I got back, I kept wishing I were still back there."

The first few nights after I was back, I woke up not sure where I was, thinking I heard my mother's voice, or my father's.

The first few days I puttered around, resuming the usual tasks and chores, and enjoying those quiet moments – folding laundry, fetching firewood, washing dishes – when memories of the past few weeks would come back to me.

Those last few times I saw my mother smile. The last time she spoke, or squeezed my hand. The way she looked, finally, after she drew her last breath; and I waited, and felt for her radial pulse, and found none; and listened with my stethoscope for her heartbeat, and heard nothing.

And how it was, in her room, after we took away all the unlovely medical supplies and paraphernalia; and she was lying there at rest, her eyes closed, in the soft light of the candles we lighted for a quiet family wake, with everyone saying goodbye for the last time before the cremation people came to take her body away, in a crimson velvet shroud.

And the quiet in the house.

People came by, for long visits, bringing food from their kitchens and flowers from their fall gardens. We kept candles burning. We drank a lot of coffee and a little wine. Every so often, out of habit I'd think, "I'd better go check on Mom." Her room seemed big and empty.

Her last days were a decline into wordlessness and pain, when narcotics were the only thing we had to work with. Looking back, I think I should have increased her medications sooner – anticipated the pain, and not allowed it to lead us. It was hard to know at the time, especially when she could no longer say what she wanted.

I'm not sure – contrary to popular belief, and to what the hospice brochure suggested – that after that point, there was anything spiritual about the process of dying. It seemed entirely physical to me, and entirely governed by pain and respiratory distress.

Had I known those details in advance, I might have asked my mother, back when she was able to answer, something like: "Mom, when would you like me to push your meds? When you can no longer speak, or swallow? When you cannot open your eyes, or feel anything but pain?" I would have asked her, "Sooner? Or later?"

I'm sure she would have told me. Exactly. It's always good to have the freedom to decide.

Her last day was one of unremitting pain, hard and troubled breathing, a ceaseless cough, and little consciousness under the heavy regimen of medications we provided. When we called the hospice people for guidance, they told us, "You can try doubling her doses of everything." We did; she seemed to relax, and find ease; and a little while later, she died.

I was, and am, thankful that the agony had ended.

Now, back home, the routines of living seem easy and familiar. The guidelines for dying are so vague. There is no accurate time frame. The pain meds can fool you into thinking that the dying person is better, at one moment; or close to death, the next. It's truly a venture into the unknown.

In much of our lives, we are generally accustomed to signs of improvement, or at least stability, rather than decline. Dying takes us by surprise; there are no gains, only losses. I would catch myself thinking, "She looks better today;" yet when other family members said those same words, I would think they were deluded. The reality was that there was no getting better, at all. That was a lesson I relearned every day, every hour, during those final weeks of my mother's life.

I'm glad I was there. I'm glad it's over. I'm glad to be back and occupied once again with life.

Revolution, Evolution

～

I think of her at odd moments.

Like when I'm standing in line at the grocery store, and I see that, among everyone with our carts and baskets loaded with beer, paper towels, Cheerios, and other household essentials, one out of three shoppers is a man.

I think of her whenever I see the words "Equal Opportunity Employer" in the classifieds. Whenever I see a woman driving a police car, a bus, or an eighteen-wheeler. Or wearing camouflage, combat boots, and armed forces insignia.

Or when the question comes up about the U.S. Presidency: Hillary, or Condoleezza? And the question is a reasonable one.

When I see women athletes, and their women coaches. When the surgeon, or the mayor, or the senator, or the department chair is a woman.

When half the people dropping their kids off at school are fathers.

Betty Friedan wasn't the only leader in the movement for equality for women who made these things possible, but it was she who most clearly described the "problem that has no name," in "The Feminine Mystique," in 1963, and chronicled our efforts, over the next three decades, to improve the status of women. She died on February 4, 2006 – her 85th birthday.

She made us look hard at our culture – at politics, at education, at the military, and especially at advertising and the media – to see how women had become, as Simone de Beauvoir put it, "the second sex." Friedan's books – rich in personal herstories – are suave analyses of the way our society regards women – and how that view has evolved. Her titles evoke our passages: "It Changed My Life," in 1976, when women first cracked the glass ceiling of employment; "The Second Stage," 1981, when we faced the next glass ceiling of power-sharing in our society (which we still have not cracked); and "The Fountain of Age," 1993, in which she analyzed the politics of aging, for women and for men.

"The Feminine Mystique" – still as outrageous as it was in 1963 – is a brazen description of the suburban-housewife cult of the postwar 1950's and '60s, when a mass-market effort took place in the media to convert middle-class women into dumbed-down consumers. Women stopped going to college in droves – attendance fell far below levels of the 1920s. They stopped reading about world and national affairs; they devoted their lives to homemaking and child-rearing. The marketing effort behind those trends is still shocking to read about. For many women, the results of the shift away from intellectual engagement to full-time wife-and-motherhood – depression, substance abuse, and financial disempowerment – were, for many, a major wake-up call, spurring the amazing, concerted efforts of hundreds of thousands of women to change the priorities of our culture during the Viet Nam era. In "Mystique," Friedan wrote a hard-hitting social history of that time.

I think of her now, when I read that one in three doctor's visits for women include a prescription for antidepressants.

Or that women are still paid 79 cents for every dollar a man earns for equivalent work. Or that shared power – in government, in education, in management – is the glass ceiling that we still have not cracked. Or that more and more women – educated, qualified – are "opting out" of the work force, withdrawing their influence, to stay home and take care of their children, because the workplace is still inhospitable, especially to women who have children.

Betty Friedan was a founder, and the first president, of the National Organization for Woman, and the National Women's Political Caucus. She was a leader in the fight for the Equal Rights Amendment, which simply said that no person shall be discriminated against on account of gender – and that this country has still refused to pass. She taught at Temple University, Yale, the New School for Social Research, Queens College, New York University and at the University of Southern California. She had three children and eight grandchildren. She had thick, wavy, undyed gray hair. She insisted that men had to be included as allies, and that the family – in whatever configuration it exists – not be rejected.

She always considered love a strong and unifying social force.

I love what she said about the evolving power of women in the world, in "The Second Stage":

> The second stage cannot be seen in terms of women alone, our separate personhood, or equality with men.
> The second stage involves coming to terms with the family – new terms with love and with work.
> The second stage may not even be a women's movement. Men may be at the cutting edge of the second stage.
> The second stage has to transcend the battle for equal power in institutions.
> The second stage will restructure institutions and transform the nature of power itself.
> The second stage may now be evolving, out of or even aside from what we have thought of as our battle.

Thank you, Betty. We'll miss you as we enter the next stage.

In Memory

It's the end of the year of my mother's death. I've been remembering the days of her passing. She spent the last month of her life in her own bed, in her own house, with her own family taking care of her. Visions of that time come to me again and again.

My friend Dr. Jane said that labor-sitting and death-sitting should be the first things that medical students are taught. I think she meant that doctors in training should learn not just the clinical phases and stages of birth and death, but to learn patience, and the art and skill of attentiveness.

My daughter, now seven, was present for the last month of her grandmother's life. At first, awed by the strange transformation of her grandmother from a lively, agile woman into a still form letting go of life, she only peeped in the doorway of the room where my mother lay in bed. The next day she came in to say hello. The day after that, she sat with her, holding her hand. Eventually she helped us turn and bathe my mother, smoothing lotion into her skin with her small warm hands.

My mother whispered, "That feels wonderful."

It was a disappointment to my mother that her doctor, the young oncologist, ended their relationship when she decided against further intervention. My mother was from the total-care era of providers, in a small town in Maine, where a doctor would see you in the hospital, stop by for a house call, then come over for a drink on Friday night. The young oncologist no longer cared for her once there were no more drugs or procedures to be bought.

I was more annoyed by the techniques he used, continuously pushing expensive treatment that was essentially useless. My father said, "They sell false hope."

My mother, at the time of her diagnosis, said, "I want chemotherapy," and was eager to try the chemotherapy that the young oncologist presented – even though the drug company's web site listed studies showing the drug's limited effectiveness and high toxicity in patients of her age and stage.

The prognosis for her kind of cancer was about four months, and there was no good reason for a terminally ill 80-year-old woman to spend part of those last months kneeling on the bathroom floor while she lost the entire lining of her GI tract – a sight the young oncologist never saw. She was so sickened and weakened by his treatment that she spent one of her precious last months in the hospital recovering from the whole-body assault, losing ground, unable to eat, instead of enjoying doing things she could have enjoyed outside.

My dad said, "They are salesmen. They overstate the benefits of the treatment, and underplay its side effects." I was surprised that any doctor in his right mind would destroy a sick person's ability to take in nutrition for the sake of selling a drug whose manufacturer's own website cited results that were, at best, dismal.

A recent story in the *Burlington Free Press* reported that this aggressive approach to chemotherapy means that ungodly numbers of end-stage cancer patients are subjected to high doses of toxic chemicals during the final weeks of their lives. You have to wonder which is the real culprit in many of these deaths: the disease or the chemotherapy.

On one hospital rotation I worked, I saw a note in a patient's chart: "She failed her chemotherapy." Shouldn't that have been the other way around? Didn't the chemotherapy fail the patient? In my mother's case, it clearly accelerated her decline.

After the first round of chemo failed, while my mother was still in the hospital recovering from its effects, the young oncologist came in and tried to sell her another, different kind of chemo. I asked him to step outside with me, and we had A Little Talk.

She's Stage 4, I told him, and according to my research there's no chemotherapy on earth that can cure that. And we've already seen what chemotherapy has done for her quality of life. The best thing you can do is to offer something supportive – vitamins, nutrients in an IV – and tell her honestly that that's the best you have for her condition.

"Oh, I don't think we can do that," he said. She went home and, of course, never saw him again.

The people who provided my family with benign, supportive treatment; with help in turning, bathing and pain relief; with psychological support and preparation for what was to come; with the blessing of their experience in end-of-life care were the women and men of the home health care and hospice groups. Their visits, for an hour or so apiece, several days a week, were helpful, though we declined the hospice's offers to sit with my mother while we did chores and errands. She would not have wanted strangers in her room during this intimate time. So it was us – my father, my sisters and brothers, my nieces and nephews – who stayed with her. Even with the difficult moment – spells of unallayed pain; daily losses of function and awareness; the mounting grief in all of us who witnessed my mother's decline – the clarity and grace of those days is something I will not soon forget.

I think often of Dr. Jane's words on the importance of attending births and deaths. I think it's a good thing that these are now occurring at home, where families can see the whole process. The more knowledgeable we all are about these passages, the more competent we will be in declaring our choices around them.

In Season

O, December's full moon casts its frostbitten glow
On my rusty old plow truck that's stuck in the snow;
The woodstove is smoking, the driveway's glare ice,
My firewood pile is a hostel for mice.
The children, all trussed in fleece hats and down coats
Are complaining of fever, earaches and sore throats.
While my partner, in slippers, and I in my clogs
Haul away stacks of seasonal bulk-mail catalogs.
Like every damn Yankee who's stuck up here freezin',
I'm progressively cranky this holiday season,
Which has gone on too long – since before Halloween;
That mass-market concept of time is obscene;
I'm beginning to wish I were born-again Jewish.
My nostrils are reddened, my fingertips bluish,
It's seasonal affective disorder time –
Let's stave off the darkness with Prozac, and rhyme.

We'll warm up the scene with a cheer and a shout
To the General we've all been thinking about –
Cheers, Martha Rainville! Hail, National Guard!
Please all come home safely, and we'll party hard.
Cheers, Debbie Salomon, Megan Moffroid,
Cindy Pierce and that doorbell we really enjoyed,
Wassail, Annie Sprinkle! Cheers, Alia Thabit,
Ann Seibert and Annie Christopher's all-natural rabbit.

For the gals at the State House we'll ring a wild bell –
Ann Cummings, Sue Bartlett, and Sara Kittell,
Ginny Lyons, Claire Ayer, and Jeanette White,
Wendy Wilton, Jane Kitchel –You light up the night!
To Hinda Miller we'll give a big hand,
And cheers to the Rippas, Barbara and Diane.
Let's bring on the bubbly! Fill up a beaker
And toast Gaye Symington, Vermont's House Speaker,

Then pause in a moment of sweet memory
For the honorable late Senator, Jean Ankeny.

Here's a mistletoe wreath with big kisses from us
To every Vermonter who got on that bus
To Ticonderoga, and the Int'l Paper plant
Where they want to burn tires – You told' em they can't!
We're dreaming up fabulous goodies to bake
For everyone trying to clean up the lake,
Like Lori Fisher and the Lake Champlain Committee,
PCB's in the drinking water are *so* not pretty.

For Vermont's civil unions! For no-fault divorce!
For Jamaica Kincaid, and Verandah Porche,
To Lisa Alther we'll give a big squeeze,
We'll applaud the Smith twins on their flying trapeze.
Cheers, Diana Barnard! Ho, Nellie Tourville,
Jill George, Patti Whitney, and Mary Z. Dill!
Bring on the band and we'll dance a wild jig
At Bear Pond, Deer Leap and the fine Flying Pig –
Cheers, indie booksellers! Cheers, ye librarians!
Progressives, feminists, and libertarians!

We'll stay up till midnight, decking and wrapping,
For whoever invented sentinel lymph node mapping.
Let's offer hosannas and hymns of praise
For the State of Vermont's forty-two CSAs,
Goose Creek! The Fat Rooster! Kildeer! and New Leaf!
Eating well without pesticides – what a relief.

Ere this holiday time becomes way too frenetic,
Let's toast the department of Molecular Biology and Genetics,
And Susan S. Wallace, the eminent chair there,
The chromosome balance appears to be fair there.
Polly Parsons chairs Medicine; Paula Tracy, Biochem;
The College of Medicine needs more like them.
Of sixteen departments, three women hold chairs now.
(Don't start me up on gender-balance affairs now.)

Season's best to Fran Stoddard, who brightens our nights,
And to Shirley Boyd-Hill, Commissioner of Human Rights,
And we'll make a gigantic musical snowman
for Cindy Fay, Pam Miller, and Mary Beth Bowman,
Jenni Johnson, the Blue Heron Renaissance Choir,
Amy Frostman, Steph Pappas, and Joann Frymire,
Robin Fawcett, and Colleen Jennings on violin,
And all of the ushers who work at the Flynn,
And to those volunteering wherever we go,
Church ladies! Fire fighters! The school PTO!

My allotment's run out, and this page is too short,
But let's not forget the Vermont Supreme Court,
Hail, Marilyn Skoglund! Hail, Denise Johnson!
We'll obey the law, and keep our long johns on.

My list's not complete; there are names I've forgot;
My cards are not written, my gifts are not bought,
But from deep in my heart, way out here in the sticks,
I wish everyone all the best in '06.

Acknowledgements

The people who helped me with these essays — who gave me ideas, quotes, funny stories, wonderful events and gatherings, hot dates, and bright ideas — are many and dear. Thanks especially to:

Jane Waterman, Diana Barnard, Willie and Stacie Baker, Marga Sproul, David Tormey, Julia Brock, Diane Magraine, Sara Packard, Natalka Slabyj, Mariana Taranto, Larry Weed, Bill Horner, Bob Bach, Bruce Leavitt, Lisa Diethelm, Scot Hill, Melissa Deas; my classmates and teachers at the University of Vermont College of Medicine; the Maternidad La Luz Birthing Center in El Paso; Penquis Family Planning, Bangor, Maine; PKC Corporation of Burlington, Vermont; the Berkeley California Women's Health Collective; and Hinesburg Family Health for a wealth of material, wisdom, and anecdotes relating to the field of health care.

Ann Hill, Susan Elias, Kren Hansen, Ruth Lamberson, Halley Ross, Connor Smith, Kim Hazelrigg, Pam Dickey, Geraldine Oppedisano, Bill Tobey, Sam Hill, Adam Purdy, Chuck Ross, and Rusty DeWees for wit, humor, good stories and funny stuff I'm glad I wrote down.

Lantman's IGA and Koval's Coffee Shop; Showtime Video and Estey Hardware; the Good Times Cafe and Papa Nick's, all wonderful places to go when you are taking a break from writing.

Natacha Pouech, Sue Barden, Elizabeth Sengle, Kathy Beyer, Roberta and Roger Soll, Ginny Roberts and Geoff Gevalt, Tim and Karen Cornish, Deirdre and Steve Gladstone, Earla Sue and Colin McNaull, the Carpenter-Carse Library Staff and Book Club, Nellie Tourville, Diane Snelling, Francy Hays, Marty Fridson, Cotton Cleveland, Nan Gladstone, Norma Hunt-Allen, Ellen Richmond, Dale Russakoff, George Nash, Walter Isaacson, Molly Hatfield, David Pitt, Laurie Waninger, Dan Swanson, Diane Shader Smith, Jeff Sagansky, Jernigan Pontiac, and my late mother, Barbara Ekemsky Hikel, who sent, lent, found, wrote, and recommended books, and who kindly read my writing from Day One.

Andrea Berger, Abigail Jones, Duane Jones, John Garvey, Martha Greenough, Ron Louie, and Steve Wisebram, friendship beyond compare.

Sue Gillis, Jan Doerler, Margaret Michniewicz, and Deb Alden of *Vermont Woman*, and Pamela Polston of *Seven Days*, who edited, arranged, and published the original versions of these essays; and Sylvie Vidrine, of Sly Dog Studio, who designed and created the cover and appearance of this book.

My dad, Rudy Hikel; my sisters Joy Hikel, Barbara Hikel, Elizabeth Jewell, Marilyn McClain, Neysa Barreto, Deana Schreindl; my brothers Jake Hikel, Dan Hikel, Jamie McCree, Al Breck; my children Cameron Hikel Breck and Jaida Claire Hikel Breck: love, fun, encouragement, and great stories.

And Walter Breck, who always said, "Keep writing! Just keep writing!"